# ORIGAMI
## Panda Family
### ~Cute Designs to Fold & Play~

# Katrin & Yuri Shumakov

# Contents

## Book Description

This is an origami panda world! ORIGAMI PANDA FAMILY will show you how to fold adorable paper pandas and the cute little environment for them! You will be able to make the origami Mama Panda and Baby Pandas, grow an origami Bamboo Forest and Cherry Blossom Trees, fold Simple Tulips and even Heart Balloons for pandas to play with. Just imagine the cute scenes of origami panda life you can create!

Do-It-Yourself - fold these wonderful and fun models, originally designed by Katrin and Yuri Shumakov. There are 450 detailed step-by-step colorful diagrams with written instructions and 105 photos of examples of completed models that will guide you through folding the 7 original origami designs and their variations. In each article, there are recommendations on paper type and size including an indication of the size of the completed model. The designs in this book are intermediate level of folding and a joy to fold and play with!

Have a creative and fun time with this book making your own Origami Panda Family!
Happy folding!

## Copyright Notice

Origami Designs, Diagrams by Yuri and Katrin Shumakov
Texts, Cover and Interior Design by Katrin and Yuri Shumakov
Photography by Katrin Shumakov

ISBN-13: 978-1499343717
ISBN-10: 149934371X

Printed by CreateSpace, An Amazon.com Company

# Introduction

This is a panda world! A cute origami panda world to be precise! You know that origami is an amazing art where we can turn ordinary sheets of paper into beautiful and intricate designs: abstract shapes, flowers, majestic castles or cute miniature pandas!

In the real world, the panda, also known as the giant panda, is a distinctive bear in a black-and-white coat native to south central China. Black patches around the eyes, over the ears, and across the round body make them stand out in the bear family. The giant pandas have lived in bamboo forests for millions of years and now are among the world's most adored and protected rare animals.

Returning to the origami world… When we started to design our pandas, we wanted them to be cute and not over complicated, so of all the tries we did we have chosen the designs where each panda is made of 2 squares - one for the head, one for the body - and they are connected by a strip without any glue. We came up with two different designs of the panda head - one to represent an adult panda and the other for a little one. So our panda designs turned out really well with quite a cartoonish look and funny facial expressions that make you want to play with them!

Soon we had the whole family of origami pandas and did their first studio photo-shoot. It happened it was a Monday and suddenly it occurred to us, "Oh, it's Panda Monday!" - sounds fun and catchy! At once we shared the Pandas picture on our Oriland Facebook page with a "Happy Panda Monday!" title (as usual we tend to share images of our new designs there). It was a huge hit and our Oriland fans loved the designs and the idea of Panda Monday itself!

Then we thought that our origami pandas need a cozy origami place to live, so we decided to create a little origami bamboo forest for them. Furthermore we grew an origami cherry blossom orchard for our pandas to enjoy. Now they needed something for fun as well, so we gave them heart balloons to play with. Since then, they are a very happy family of origami pandas!

We hope you will enjoy this book, having a pandastic experience with all the designs presented here and make your own Origami Panda Family! Happy folding!

*The Authors,*
*Katrin and Yuri Shumakov*

*Join origami Panda Monday fun! Come to our Oriland's Facebook and share pictures of your origami pandas with all Oriland friends!*
*https://www.facebook.com/oriland.fb*

# Gallery

Mama Panda
**p. 7**

Baby Panda
**p. 28**

Origami Panda Family

Bamboo
**p. 51**

Flower Holder
**p. 59**

Cherry Blossom Tree
**p. 63**

Simple Tulip
**p. 72**

Heart Balloon
**p. 75**

# Origami Symbols

These simple origami symbols will help you to read diagrams of folding - they show the direction in which the paper has to be folded. Look at the diagram to note which way the lines and arrows - all the symbols demonstrate, and fold your paper according to the diagram. To learn more about origami basics, please visit Oriversity section at our Oriland.com site.

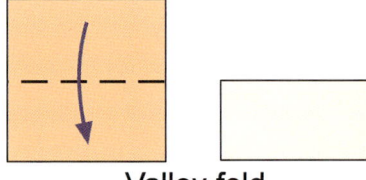

Valley fold

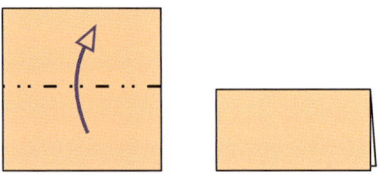

Mountain fold

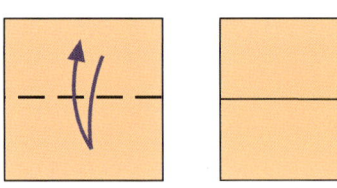

Valley fold and unfold

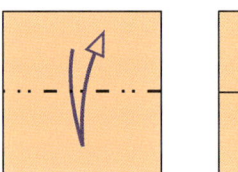

Mountain fold and unfold

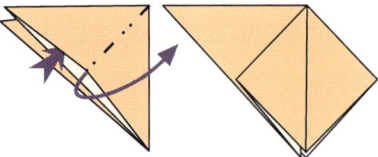

Open and squash

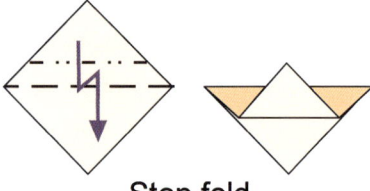

Step fold

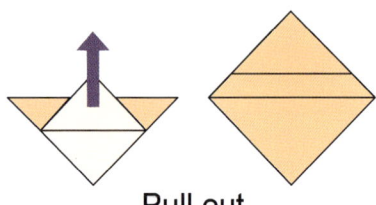

Pull out

Push in. Sink

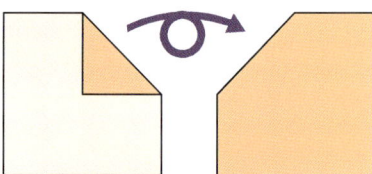

Turn the paper over

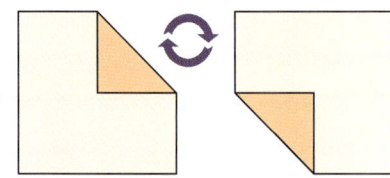

Turn the paper around

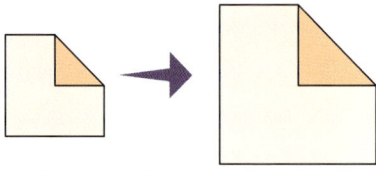

Following diagram is enlarged

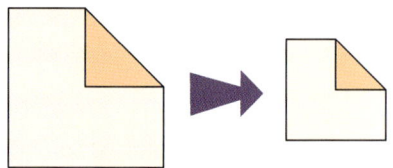

Following diagram is reduced

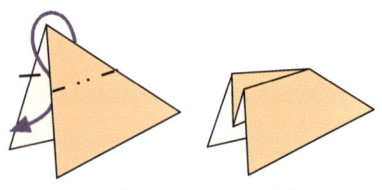

Inside reverse fold

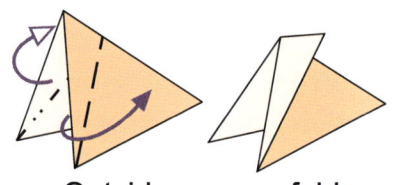

Outside reverse fold

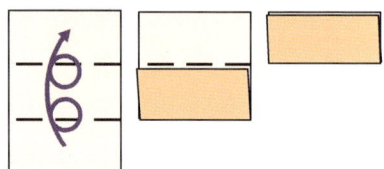

Fold the paper over and over

X-ray view    ·················

## Helpful Tips

- Fold the paper on a smooth surface with good lighting.
- Move step by step and don't skip over the next diagram.
- While folding, it's good to pay attention to the diagram of the following step, where the result of the folding is shown.
- After the step is done, don't forget to turn the model into the position shown in the next diagram.
- Smooth out the creases carefully, do not make unnecessary folds.
- If you become confused with the diagrams, don't panic! Study previous steps and see if you missed something. Also, it might be a good idea to start anew.
    And most importantly, have fun!

## Level of folding

⭐ Simple
⭐⭐ Simple-Medium
⭐⭐⭐ Medium
⭐⭐⭐⭐ Medium-Complex
⭐⭐⭐⭐⭐ Complex

The system of levels of folding is more like a guideline and mostly depends of your skills in paper folding. If you are a novice, even the simple level can be challenging for you. And if you are already a connoisseur even a complex model can be simple for you.

# Mama Panda
## by Katrin & Yuri Shumakov

This cute design of Mama Panda folds from 2 squares used for the head and the body. A strip, 1:4 in proportion, will be needed to connect two parts together with paper locks without any glue. You will be able to adjust the position of the body and the head to your liking.

**Suggested paper:** Regular origami paper.

**Suggested sizes:** Use two 6-inch (15 cm) squares and a strip 1-1/2x6 inches (3.75x15cm). Or two 5-inch (12.5 cm) squares and a strip 1-1/4x5 inches (3x12.5cm). When you master the model, you can use smaller paper like 3-inch (7.5cm) squares.

**Suggested colors:** It's natural to use two-color paper in black and white.

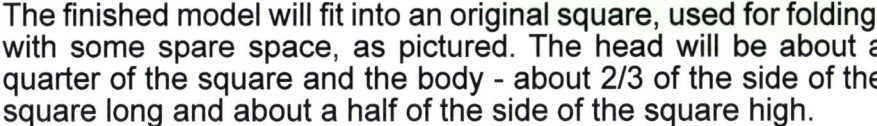

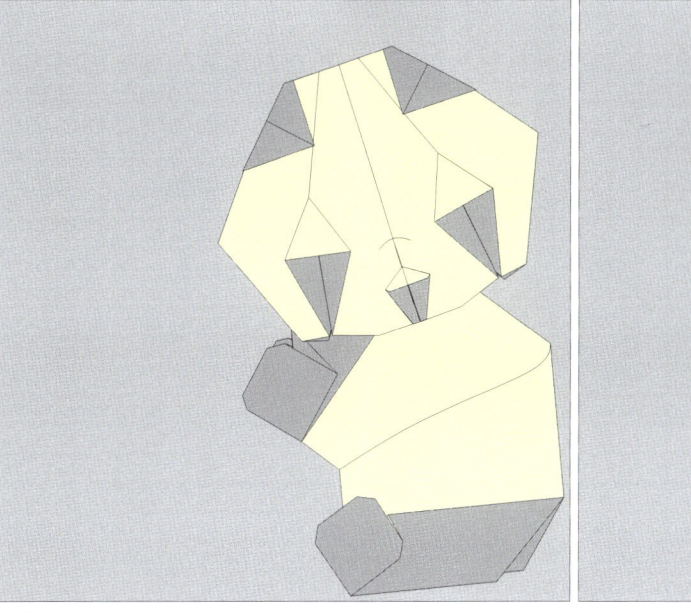

The finished model will fit into an original square, used for folding, with some spare space, as pictured. The head will be about a quarter of the square and the body - about 2/3 of the side of the square long and about a half of the side of the square high.

Mama Panda © 2013 Katrin and Yuri Shumakov

# Mama Panda Head

Take a square of paper.

*Begin with colored side up.*

Valley fold the opposite corners together in turn to mark the diagonal fold lines, and open them up. Turn the paper over.

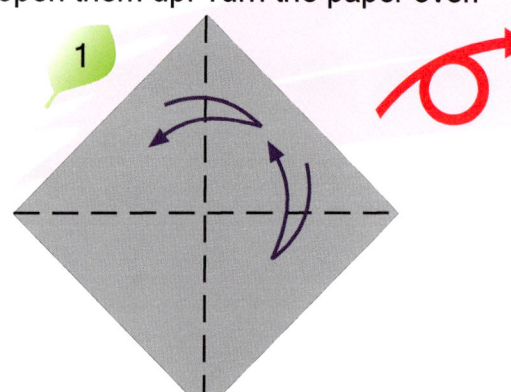

Valley fold the opposite sides together in both directions, and open them up.

Working with the front flaps, valley fold the upper right-hand sloping edge over to meet the vertical middle line, as shown. Press it flat. Repeat with the left-hand sloping edge.

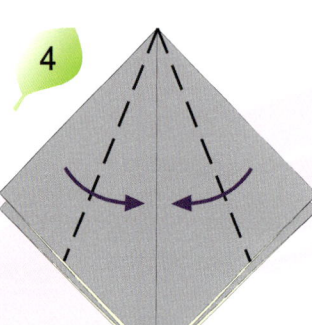

Bring the sides together and down towards you. Press the top down neatly into a square, thereby completing the shape that in origami is called the preliminary or square base.

This should be the result. Turn the model over from side to side.

Working with the front thin triangular flaps, bring the bottom edge of the right-hand flap to the right into the vertical position as shown by the dotted line. Note the fold-line is passing through the side corner. Repeat with the left-hand triangular flap.

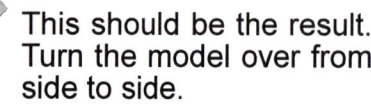

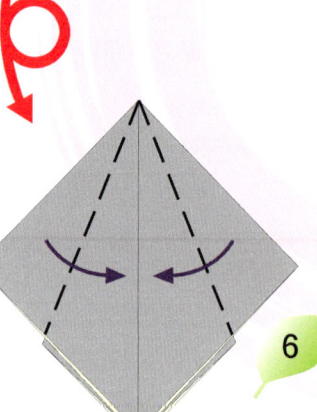

Repeat step 4 for this side as well.

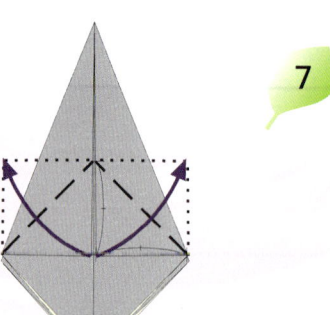

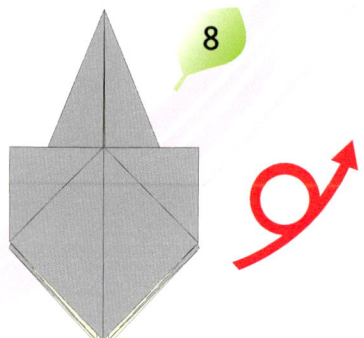

This should be the result. Turn the model over from side to side.

Mama Panda © 2013 Katrin and Yuri Shumakov

Origami Panda Family

Working with the front thin triangular flaps, valley fold the right-hand flap to meet the side edge of the back flap. Repeat with the left-hand triangular flap.

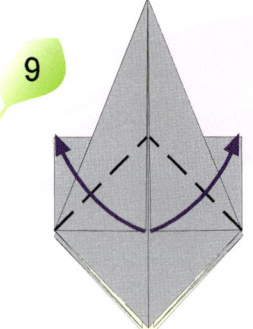

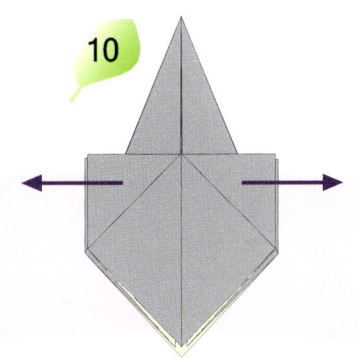

Open the side flaps out. Repeat behind.

Now open the paper completely.

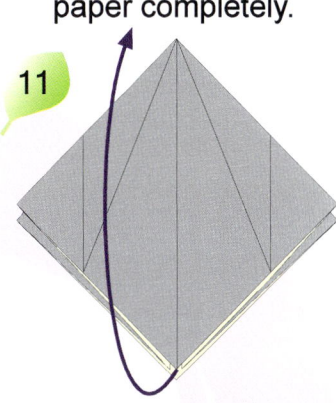

This should be the result. Turn the paper over and around into the position shown in the next step.

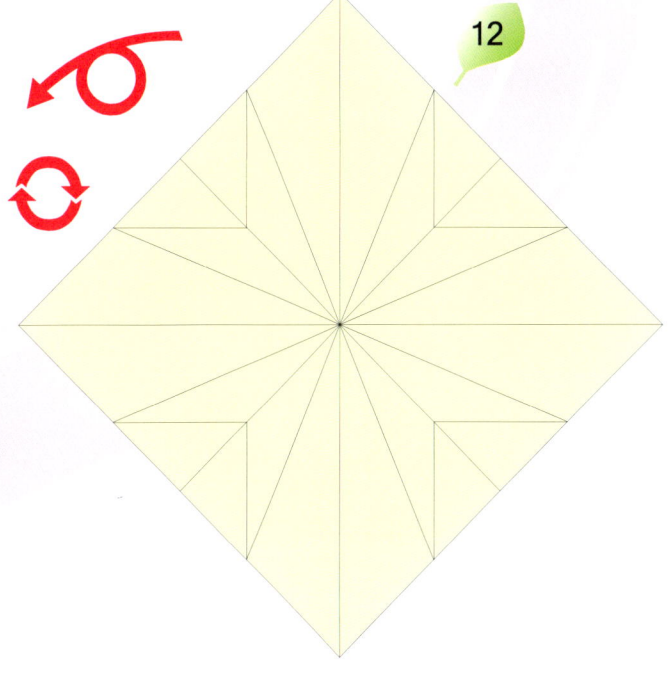

Bring the sides together and down towards you. Press the top down neatly into a triangle, thereby completing the shape that in origami is called the balloon base.

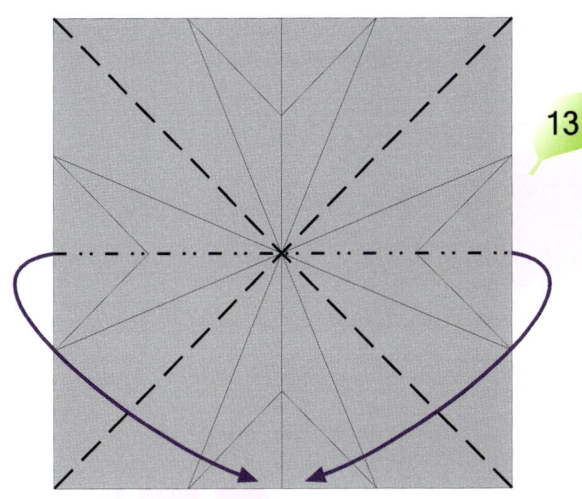

Now valley fold the narrow right-hand flap to the left, as if turning the page of a book.

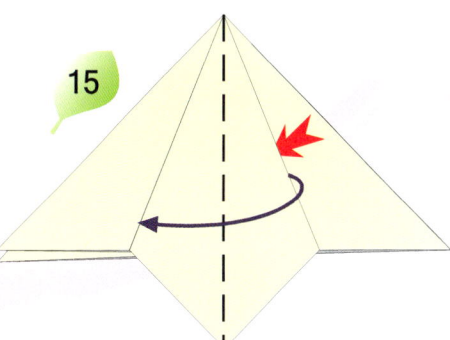

Working with the right-hand flap, turn it half-way to the left as if you are turning the page of a book, at the same time separate the layers of this flap from the bottom and squash the flap down neatly into the position shown in the next step.

Mama Panda © 2013 Katrin and Yuri Shumakov

Separate the front layer and along the existing fold-lines form 'valleys' as shown.

**16**

**17** Lift the bottom edge of the front layer up, thereby making a tent-like fold, at the same time valley folding the flap over to the right.

**19** This should be the result. Now turn the model over from side to side.

**18** This should be the result. Now valley fold the narrow left-hand flap to the right, as if turning the page of a book. Then repeat steps 16-17 as in mirror.

**20** Repeat steps 14 to 18 for this side.

**21** Working with the front layer, valley fold the bottom corner up as shown.

**22** Separate the front flap and fold it up as far as it will go.

**23** This should be the result. Mountain fold the left- and right-hand corners of the front flap along the edges of the back layers, thereby forming the ears on the other side.

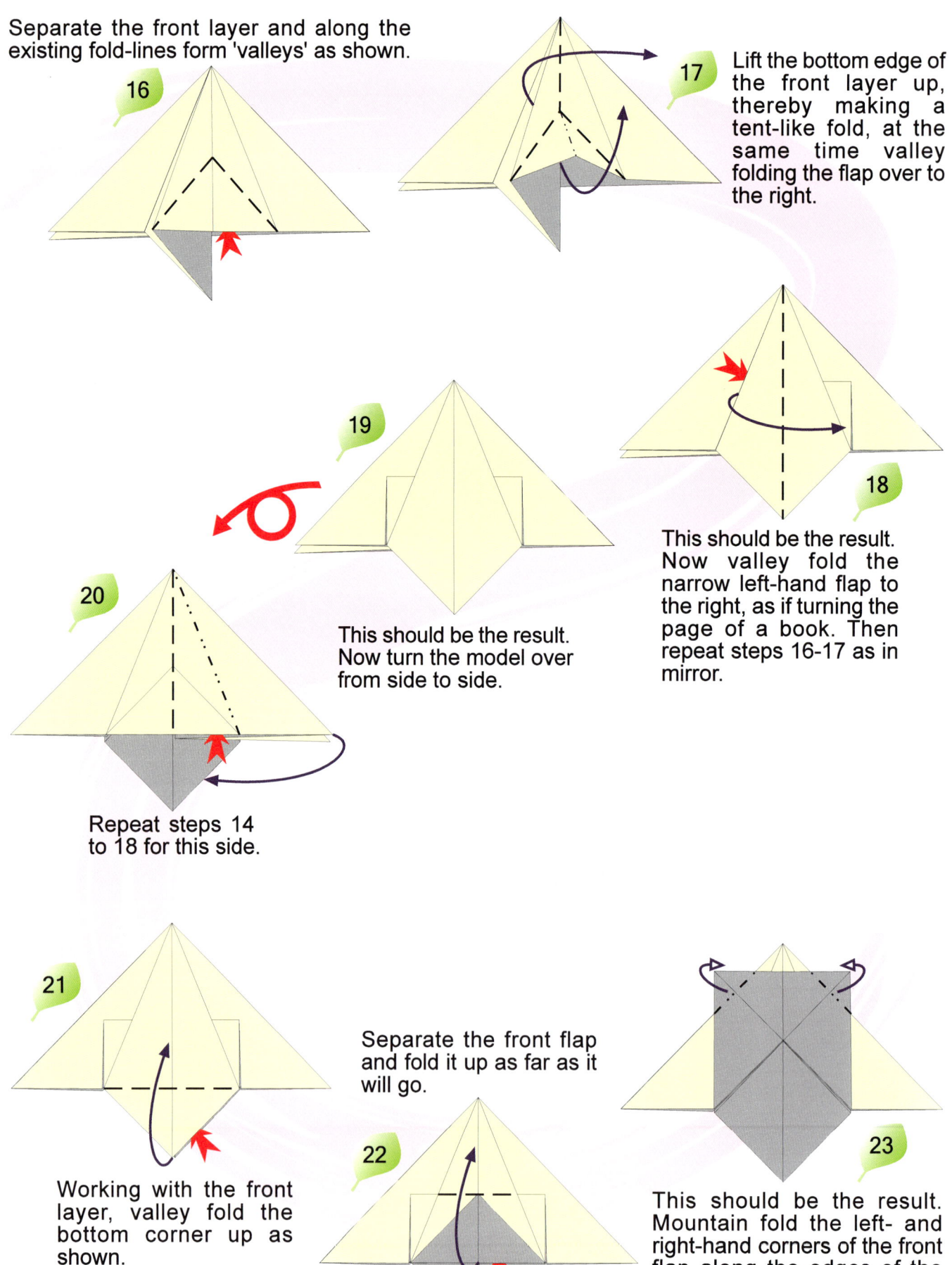

Mama Panda © 2013 Katrin and Yuri Shumakov

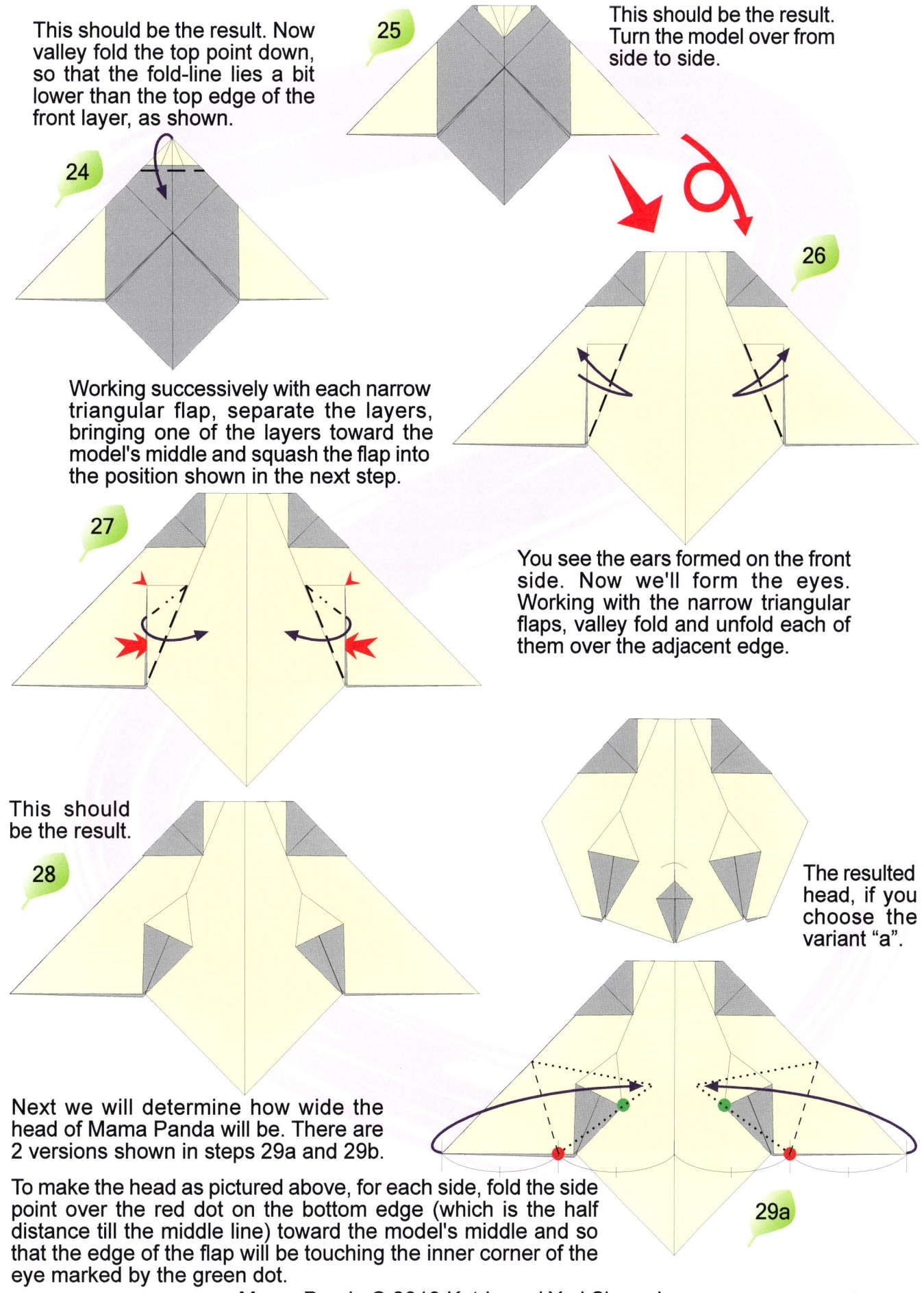

This should be the result. Now valley fold the top point down, so that the fold-line lies a bit lower than the top edge of the front layer, as shown.

24

25

This should be the result. Turn the model over from side to side.

26

Working successively with each narrow triangular flap, separate the layers, bringing one of the layers toward the model's middle and squash the flap into the position shown in the next step.

27

You see the ears formed on the front side. Now we'll form the eyes. Working with the narrow triangular flaps, valley fold and unfold each of them over the adjacent edge.

This should be the result.

28

The resulted head, if you choose the variant "a".

Next we will determine how wide the head of Mama Panda will be. There are 2 versions shown in steps 29a and 29b.

To make the head as pictured above, for each side, fold the side point over the red dot on the bottom edge (which is the half distance till the middle line) toward the model's middle and so that the edge of the flap will be touching the inner corner of the eye marked by the green dot.

29a

Mama Panda © 2013 Katrin and Yuri Shumakov

The further steps shown on an example of the variant "a", but note whichever variant you choose to do "a" or "b", except minor difference in proportion, the next steps are the same.

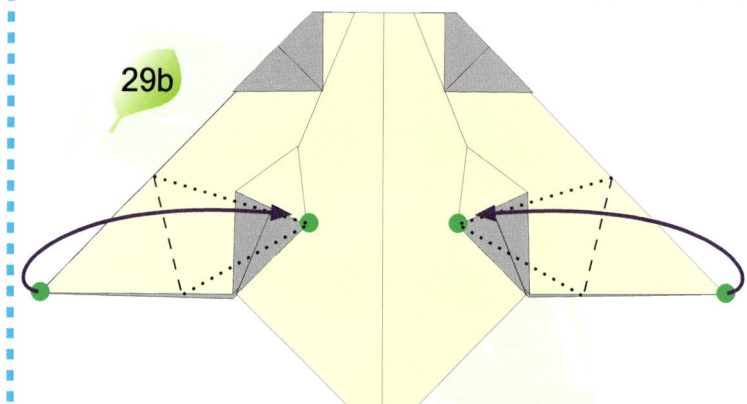

29b

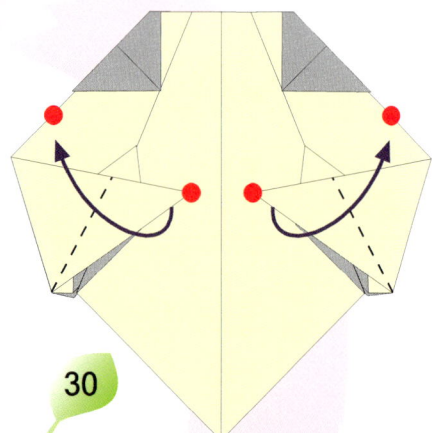

30

To make a wider (more cartoon-like) head as pictured, fold the side point over toward the model's middle to meet the inner corner of the eye, so that the green dots coincide.

Working successively with each triangular flap, valley fold the marked point of the flap to meet the upper sloping edge as shown, so the dots coincide. Note the fold-line should start at the lower point of the flap.

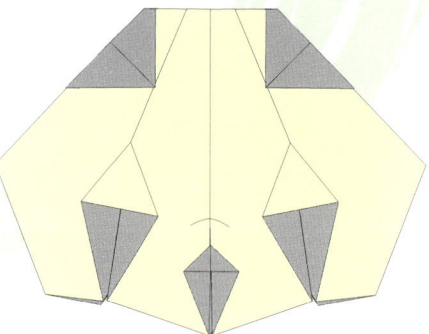

The resulted head, if you choose the variant "b".

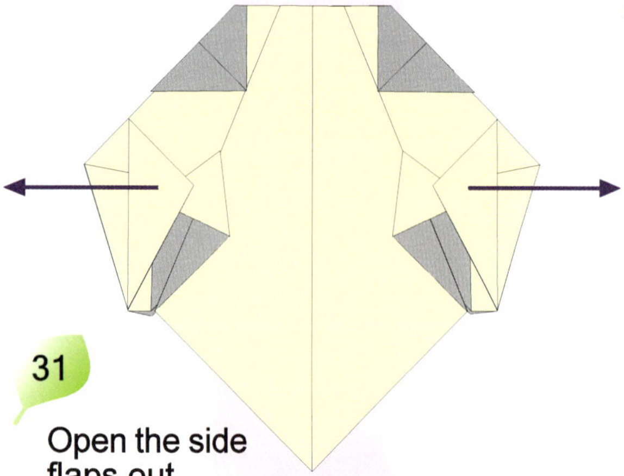

31

Open the side flaps out.

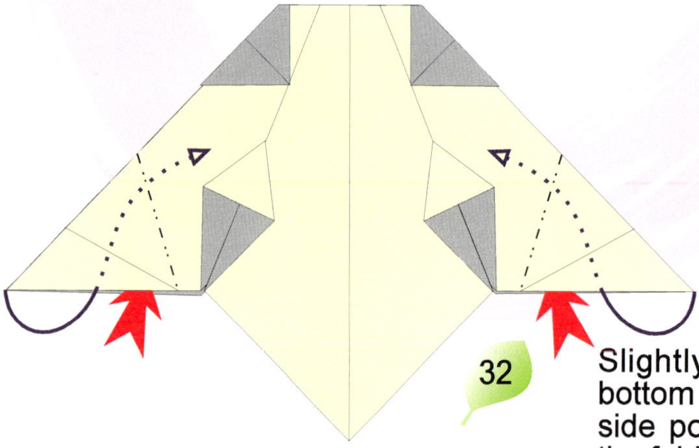

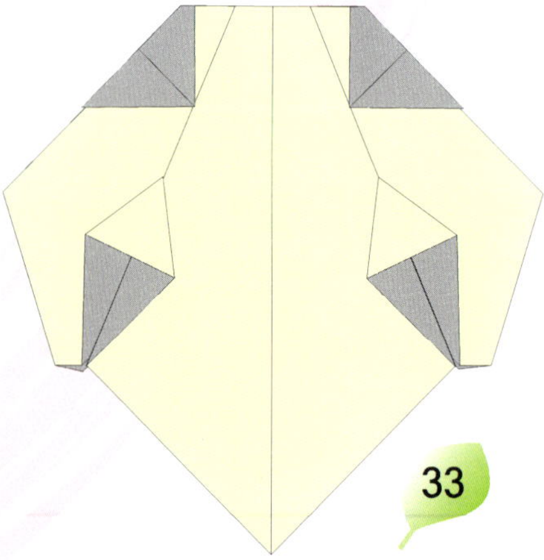

33

This should be the result.

32

Slightly open the layers at the bottom and inside reverse fold the side points into the model along the fold-lines you did in step 29.

Mama Panda © 2013 Katrin and Yuri Shumakov

Inside the model, along the existing fold-lines valley fold the triangular flap, thereby locking one side of the head.

**34**

View through the front layer.

**35**

This should be the result. Now lock the other side in the same way.

View through the front layer.

As the model is locked on sides now, insert fingers inside as if sliding them into the pocket and separate the front layers from the back ones, thereby opening the model slightly.

**36**

The top point of the flap has to be approximately on the level of the inner corners of the eyes and the side point - about a half of the lower sloping edge.

There is no strict proportion to how big this inner flap should be, small deviations from the shown guide-lines will result in unique facial features of your origami panda.

**37**

Now pinch the lower part of the vertical middle line from the inside, and bring it as a flap to the right, thereby shaping the dart-like fold as shown in the next step.

It's like a straight dart in sewing.

**38**

Fold and unfold the inner flap to the left, marking its middle vertical fold-line on the left-hand side. Then release the flap.

Now lift the lower part of the dart up as shown, it will be the nose part, and fold the dart-like flap inside to the right while the nose part remains visible at the left side.

**39**

**40**

This should be the result. Keep the inner flap and the front layer compressed at the place shown by the circle.

Mama Panda © 2013 Katrin and Yuri Shumakov

Keeping the inner flap and the front layer compressed, open the layers of the nose part and squash the top point into a quadrangle as shown in the next step.

41

42

While keeping the inner flap and the front layer compressed, fold the corner of the small quadrangle flap up as shown, thereby forming Panda's nose.

43

This should be the result. Turn the model over from side to side, keeping the inner flap and the front layer compressed.

44

Mountain fold the left-hand lower sloping edge of the flap, thereby locking it securely in the place.

45

This should be the result. Turn the model over from side to side.

You may adjust a few details for a different appearance.

46

This should be the result. The head for Mama Panda is ready!

47

Mountain fold the lower point, thereby making the face more round.

48

This should be the result - the head with the round chin line.

Mama Panda © 2013 Katrin and Yuri Shumakov

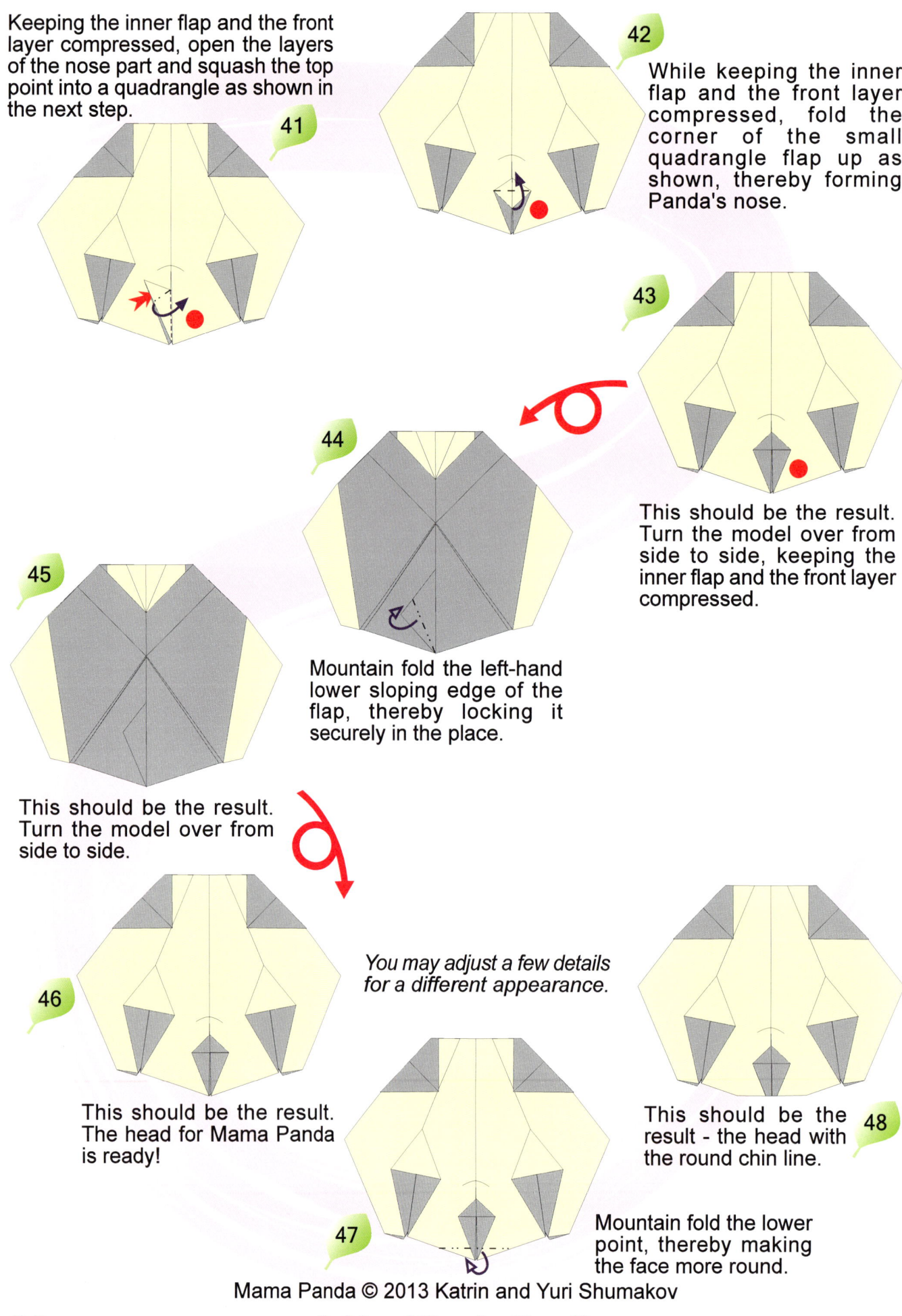

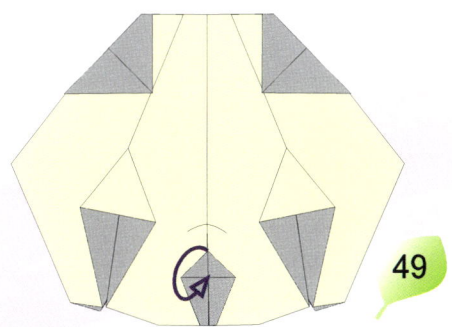

49

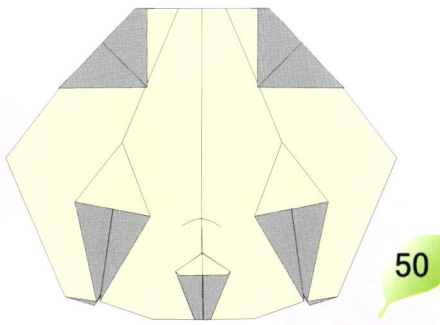

50

Another adjustment can be made for the nose part. Unfold the small flap of the nose and insert its tip under itself as far as it will go.

This should be the result. Here is the completed head for Mama Panda with the round chin and the adjusted nose.

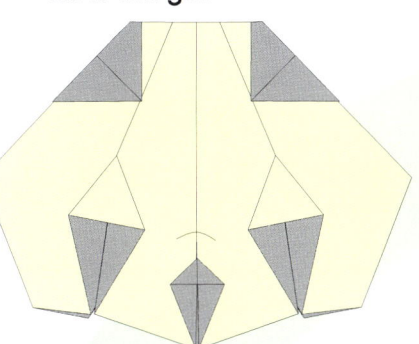

Wide Head, Pointy Chin

Regular Head, Pointy Chin

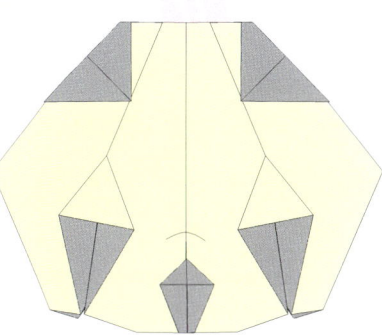

Regular Head, Round Chin

Wide Head, Round Chin

You can make various adjustments during folding to have a different appearance of the head, so that each Panda will be unique.

Wide Head, Pointy Chin

Regular Head, Pointy Chin, Adjusted Nose

Back Side

Regular Head, Pointy Chin

Mama Panda © 2013 Katrin and Yuri Shumakov

# Panda Body

Take a square identical in size to the paper square used for the head.

*Begin with colored side up.*

Valley fold the opposite corners together in turn to mark the diagonal fold lines, and open them up. Turn the paper over.

**1**

**2** Valley fold the top and bottom edges to meet the horizontal middle-line. Press them flat and unfold them.

**3** Valley fold the top and bottom edges to meet the fold-lines made in step 2. Press them flat.

**4** This should be the result. Then turn the paper over and around into the position shown in the next step.

**5** Fold and unfold each of the corners as shown, but don't press the fold completely flat just making a mark on the side edge.

**6** Valley fold the top and bottom edges being guided by the fold-marks made in step 5. Press them flat.

**7** This should be the result. Unfold the flaps.

**8** Valley fold the top half of the model down.

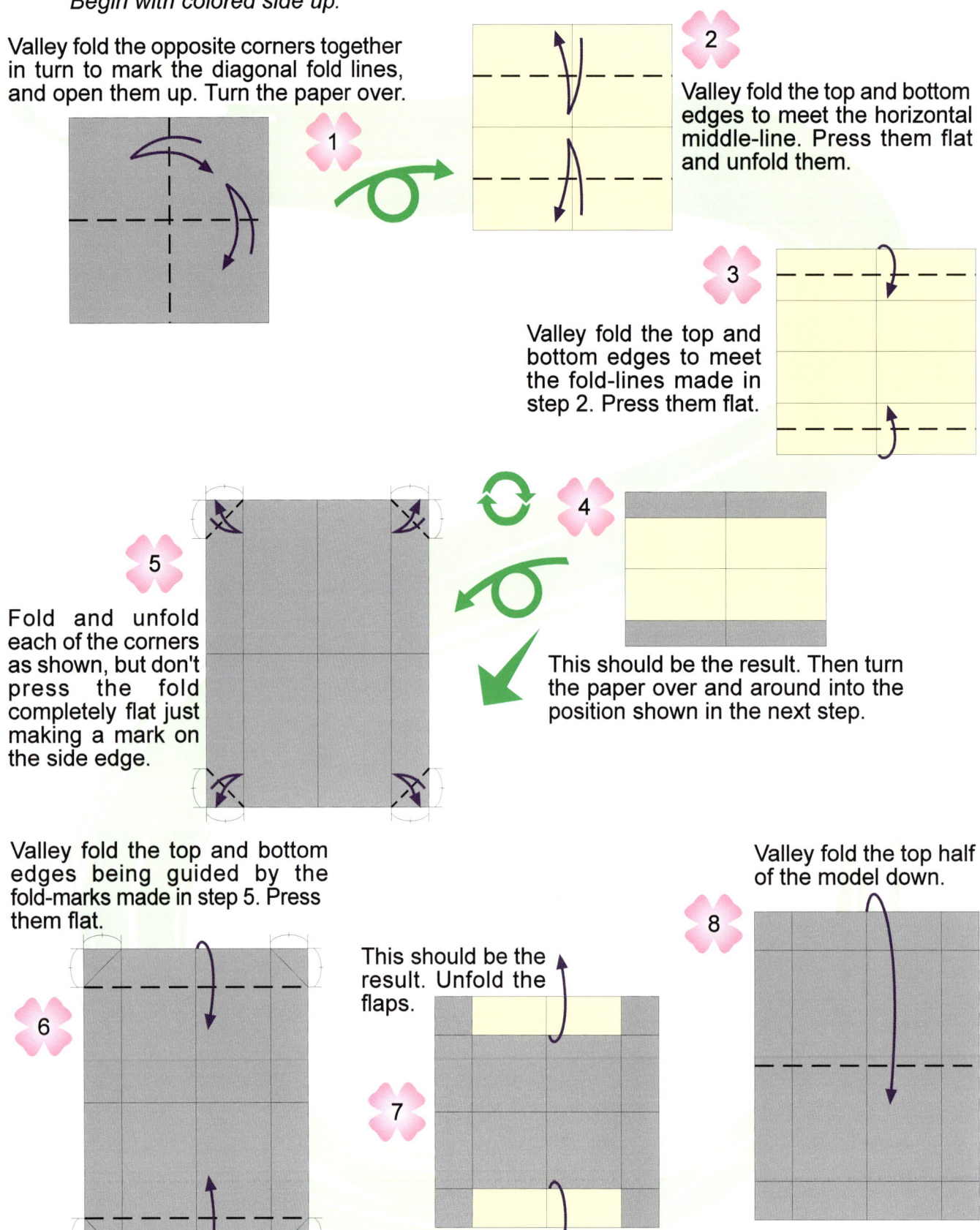

Mama Panda © 2013 Katrin and Yuri Shumakov

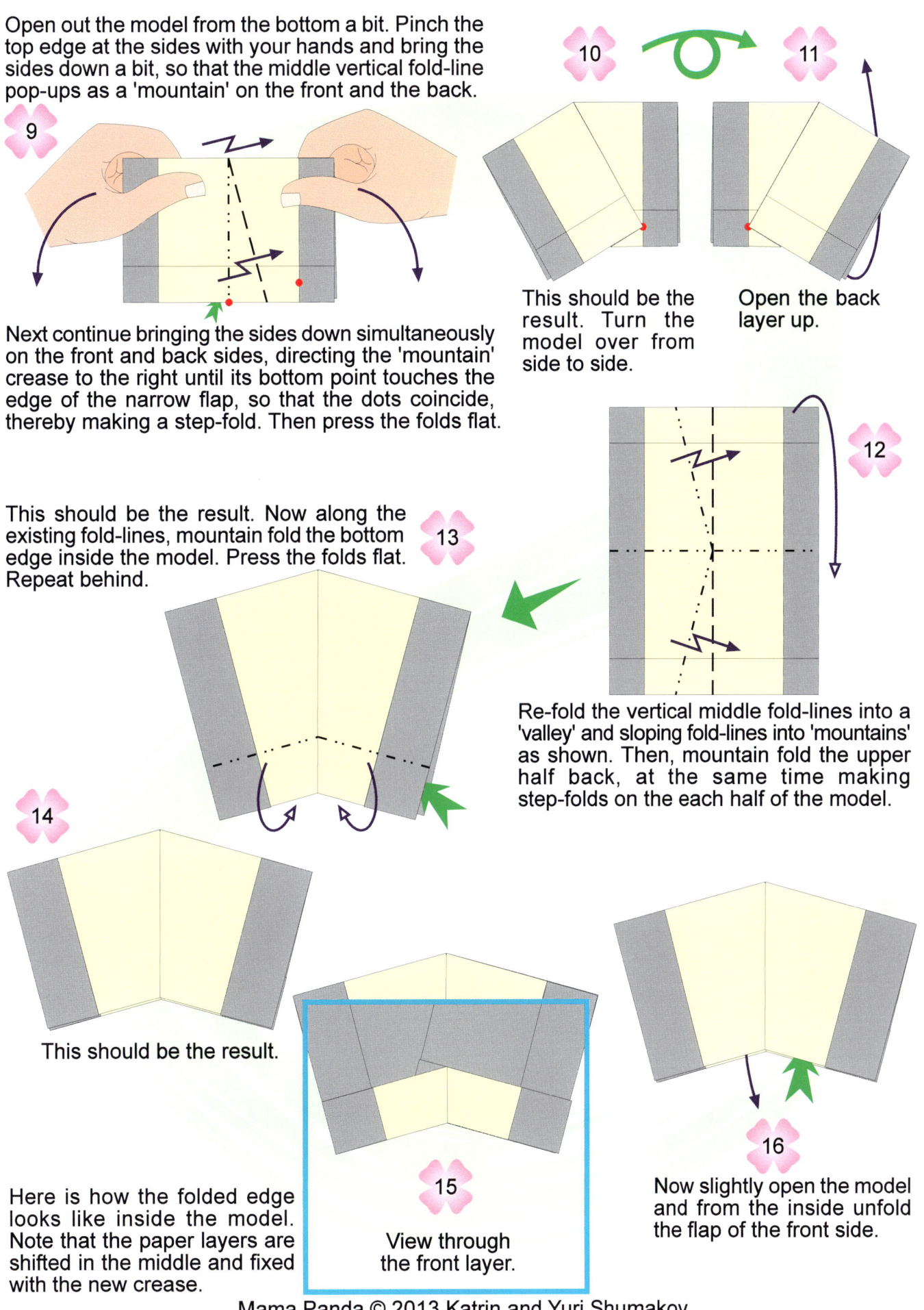

Open out the model from the bottom a bit. Pinch the top edge at the sides with your hands and bring the sides down a bit, so that the middle vertical fold-line pop-ups as a 'mountain' on the front and the back.

**9**

Next continue bringing the sides down simultaneously on the front and back sides, directing the 'mountain' crease to the right until its bottom point touches the edge of the narrow flap, so that the dots coincide, thereby making a step-fold. Then press the folds flat.

**10** **11**

This should be the result. Turn the model over from side to side.

Open the back layer up.

**12**

Re-fold the vertical middle fold-lines into a 'valley' and sloping fold-lines into 'mountains' as shown. Then, mountain fold the upper half back, at the same time making step-folds on the each half of the model.

This should be the result. Now along the existing fold-lines, mountain fold the bottom edge inside the model. Press the folds flat. Repeat behind.

**13**

**14**

This should be the result.

Here is how the folded edge looks like inside the model. Note that the paper layers are shifted in the middle and fixed with the new crease.

**15**

View through the front layer.

**16**

Now slightly open the model and from the inside unfold the flap of the front side.

Mama Panda © 2013 Katrin and Yuri Shumakov

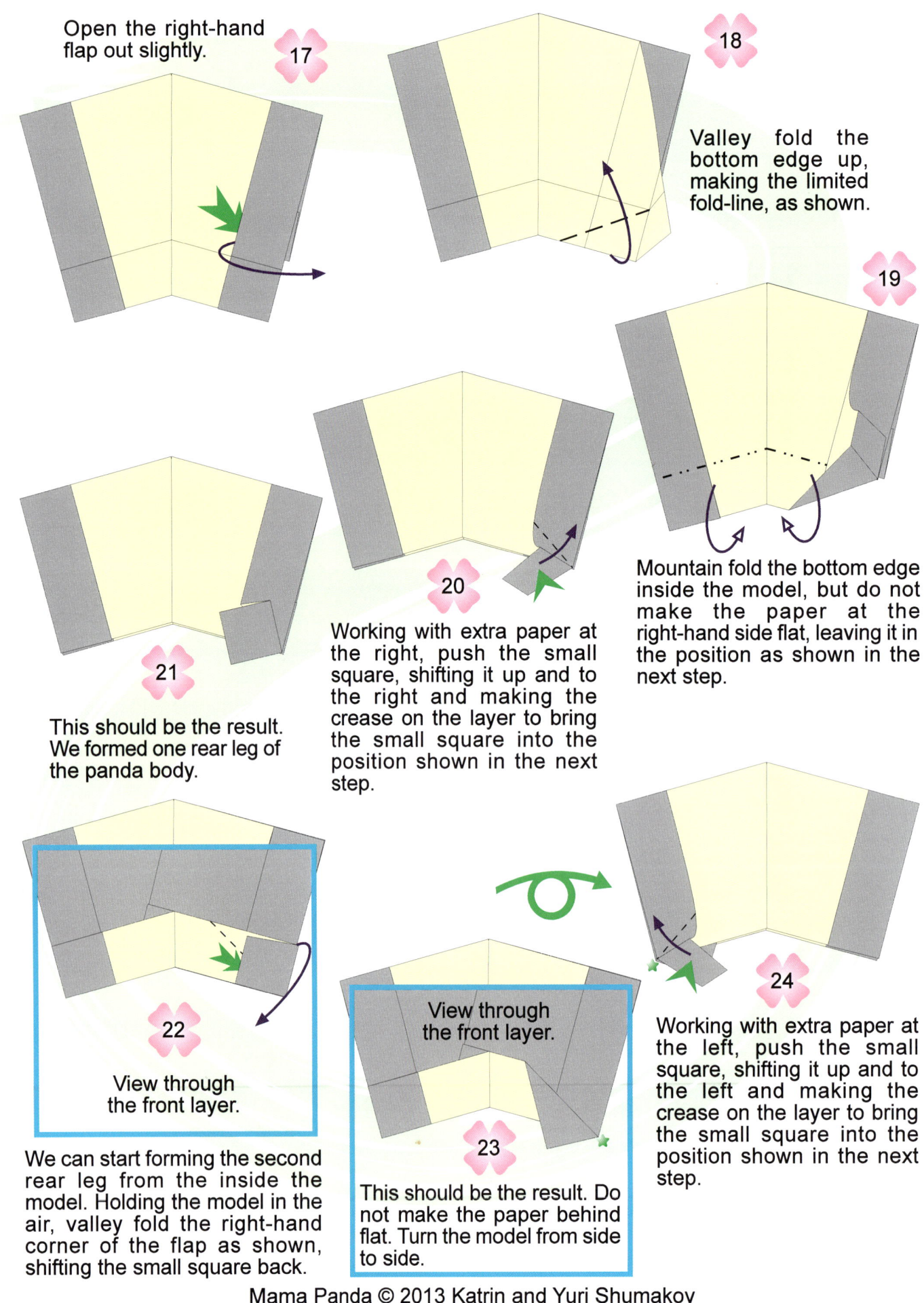

Open the right-hand flap out slightly.

**17**

**18**

Valley fold the bottom edge up, making the limited fold-line, as shown.

**19**

Mountain fold the bottom edge inside the model, but do not make the paper at the right-hand side flat, leaving it in the position as shown in the next step.

**20**

Working with extra paper at the right, push the small square, shifting it up and to the right and making the crease on the layer to bring the small square into the position shown in the next step.

**21**

This should be the result. We formed one rear leg of the panda body.

**22**

View through the front layer.

We can start forming the second rear leg from the inside the model. Holding the model in the air, valley fold the right-hand corner of the flap as shown, shifting the small square back.

**23**

View through the front layer.

This should be the result. Do not make the paper behind flat. Turn the model from side to side.

**24**

Working with extra paper at the left, push the small square, shifting it up and to the left and making the crease on the layer to bring the small square into the position shown in the next step.

Mama Panda © 2013 Katrin and Yuri Shumakov

This should be the result - the second rear leg is formed.

25

Now we will form the front legs.

View through the front layer.

26

Note the small square on the inside flap. Separate the layer a bit. Repeat the same with the inside flap of the front layer.

Open the model slightly at the right, pinch the lower corner and valley fold it as shown, at the same time bring the small square flap from the inside, so that it shifts atop all the layers.

27

28

This should be the result. Turn the model over from side to side.

Open the model slightly at the left, pinch the lower corner and valley fold it as shown, at the same time bring the small square flap from the inside, so that it shifts atop all the layers.

29

This should be the result.

30

Working inside the model, pinch the left-hand side of the flap as shown and move it a bit down and aside into the position shown in the next step. At the same time let the layer stretch in the middle of the flap, shifting and fixing it with the new crease. Then smooth the paper on this flap to fix the new position.

View through the front layer.

31

View through the front layer.

32

This should be the result. Turn the model over from side to side.

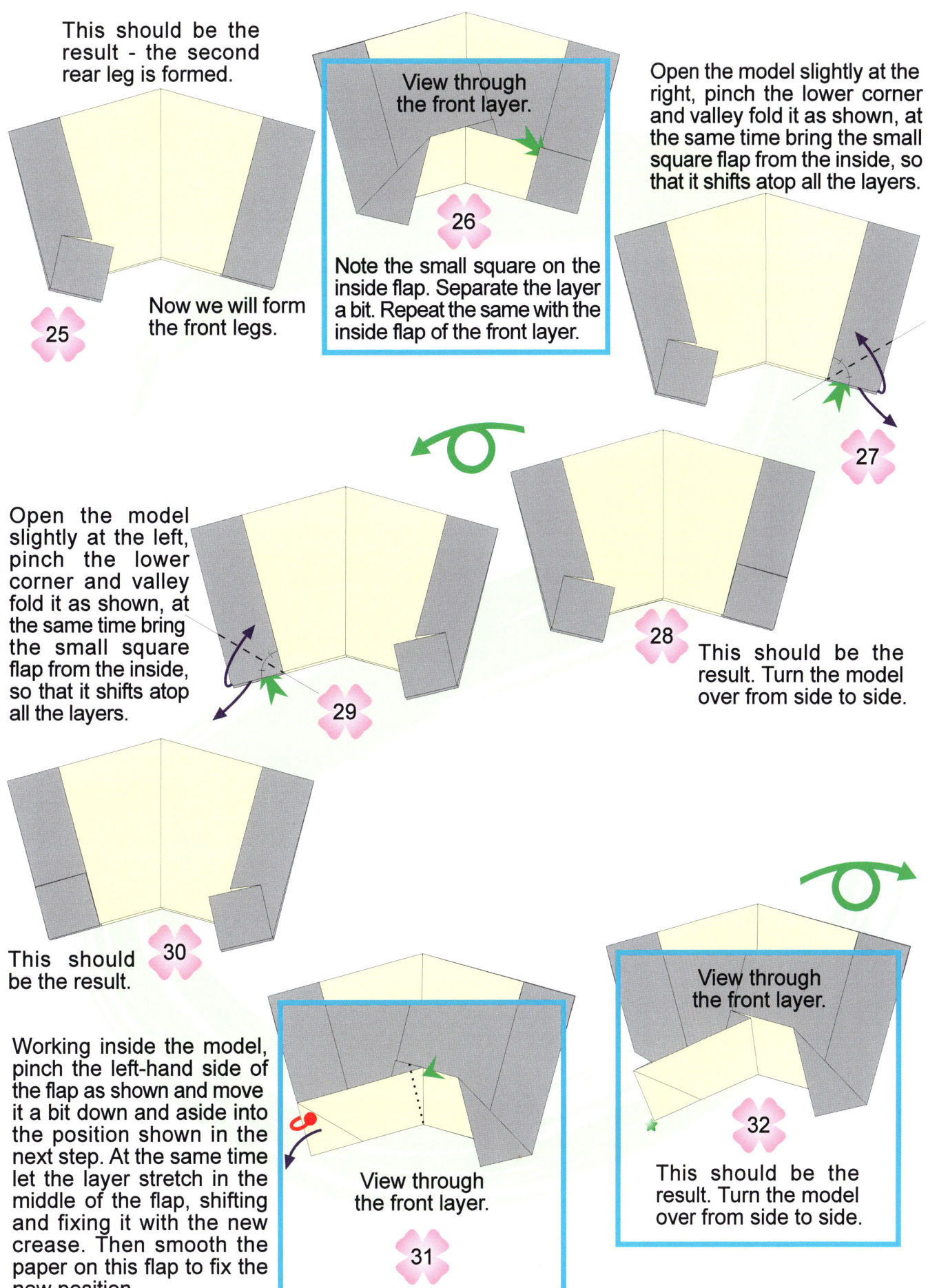

Mama Panda © 2013 Katrin and Yuri Shumakov

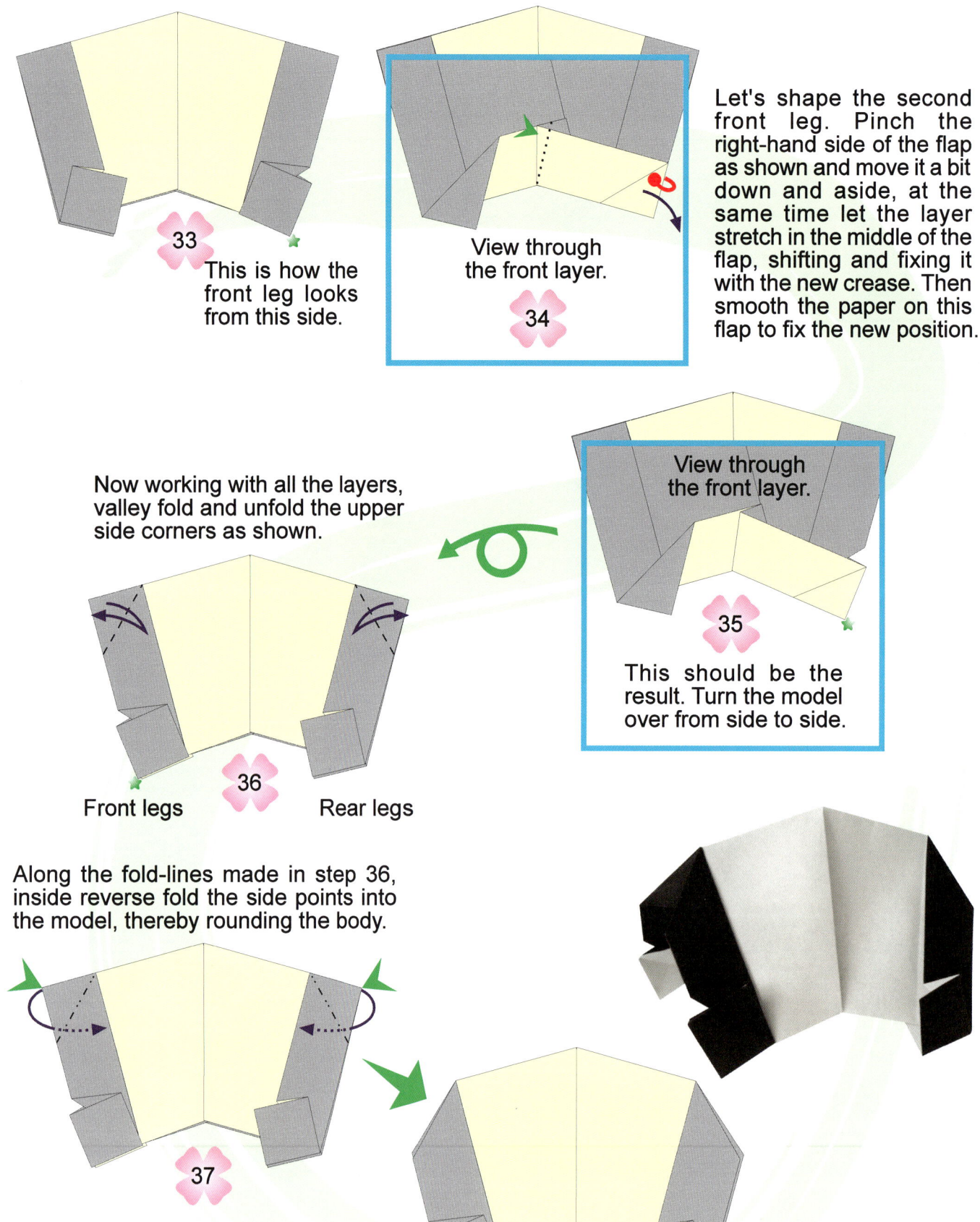

**33**

This is how the front leg looks from this side.

View through the front layer.

**34**

Let's shape the second front leg. Pinch the right-hand side of the flap as shown and move it a bit down and aside, at the same time let the layer stretch in the middle of the flap, shifting and fixing it with the new crease. Then smooth the paper on this flap to fix the new position.

View through the front layer.

**35**

This should be the result. Turn the model over from side to side.

Now working with all the layers, valley fold and unfold the upper side corners as shown.

**36**

Front legs          Rear legs

Along the fold-lines made in step 36, inside reverse fold the side points into the model, thereby rounding the body.

**37**

**38**

The Panda Body is ready!

Mama Panda © 2013 Katrin and Yuri Shumakov

Here is the Panda Body
in the sitting position.

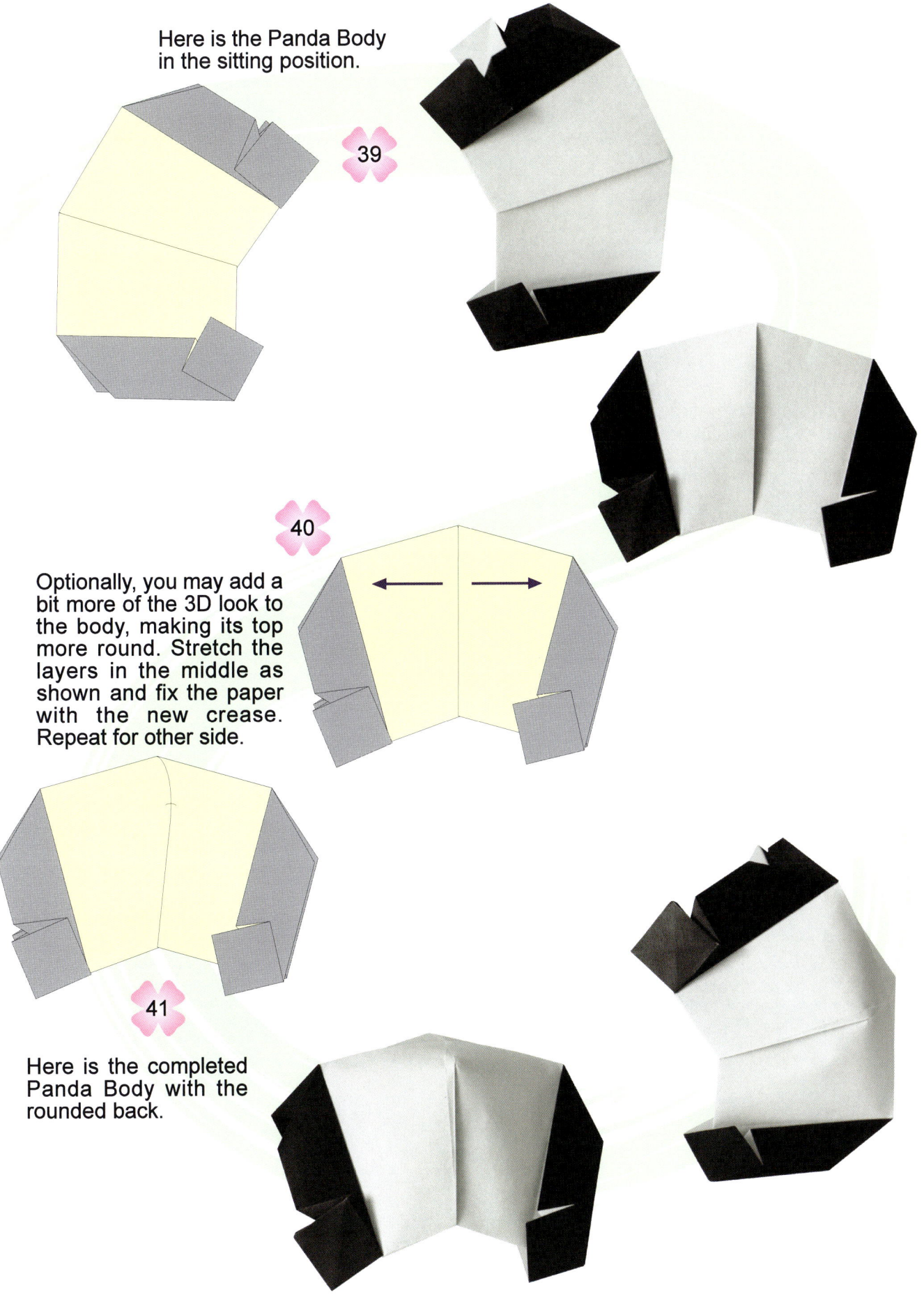

**39**

**40**

Optionally, you may add a
bit more of the 3D look to
the body, making its top
more round. Stretch the
layers in the middle as
shown and fix the paper
with the new crease.
Repeat for other side.

**41**

Here is the completed
Panda Body with the
rounded back.

Mama Panda © 2013 Katrin and Yuri Shumakov

# Panda Tubby Body

Basing on the main design of the panda body, we can make its tubby variation. Use a square identical in size to the paper square used for the head. Follow diagrams shown on page 16 to fold the first 8 steps.

**9**

Open-out the model from the bottom a bit. Pinch the top edge at the sides with your hands and bring the sides down a bit, so that the middle vertical fold-line pop-up as a 'mountain' on the front and the back. Direct the 'mountain' crease on both sides to the right until its bottom point touches the edge, so that the dots coincide. Then press the folds flat.

**10**

This should be the result. Turn the model over from side to side.

**11**

Open the back layer up.

This should be the result. Now along the existing fold-lines, mountain fold the bottom edge inside the model. Press the folds flat. Repeat behind.

**13**

This should be the result.

**12**

Re-fold the vertical middle fold-lines into a 'valley' and sloping fold-lines into 'mountains' as shown. Then, mountain fold the upper half back, at the same time making step-folds on the each half of the model.

**14**

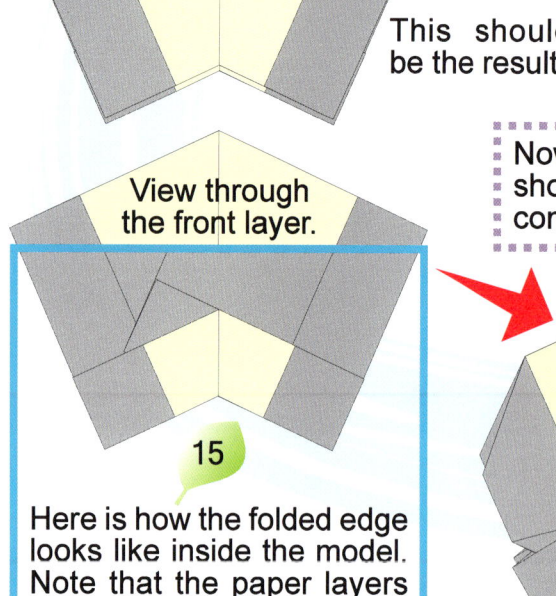

View through the front layer.

**15**

Here is how the folded edge looks like inside the model. Note that the paper layers are shifted in the middle and fixed with the new crease.

Now follow steps 16 to 38 shown on pages 17-20 to complete the model.

**38**

**39**

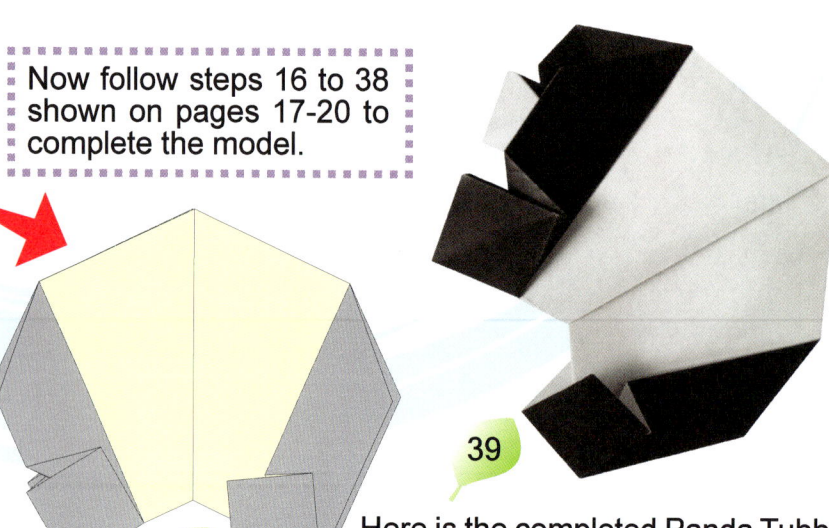

Here is the completed Panda Tubby Body, which can be put in the sitting position too.

Mama Panda © 2013 Katrin and Yuri Shumakov

# Connector

This connector will be used to unite the Panda Head and Body together without any glue. Use a strip, 1:4 in proportion, which is 1/4 of the original square used for the head or body.

*Begin with colored side up.*

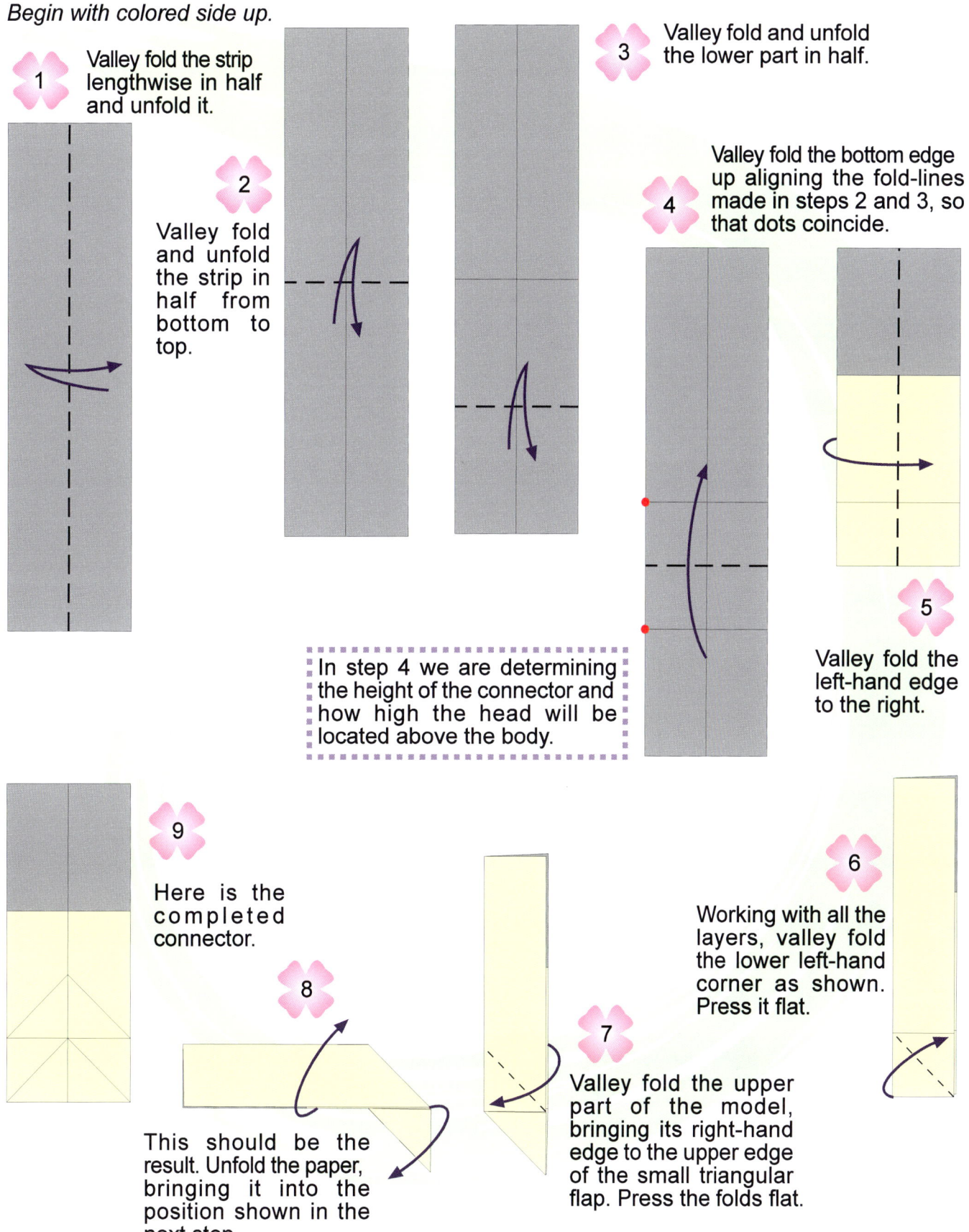

**1** Valley fold the strip lengthwise in half and unfold it.

**2** Valley fold and unfold the strip in half from bottom to top.

**3** Valley fold and unfold the lower part in half.

**4** Valley fold the bottom edge up aligning the fold-lines made in steps 2 and 3, so that dots coincide.

In step 4 we are determining the height of the connector and how high the head will be located above the body.

**5** Valley fold the left-hand edge to the right.

**6** Working with all the layers, valley fold the lower left-hand corner as shown. Press it flat.

**7** Valley fold the upper part of the model, bringing its right-hand edge to the upper edge of the small triangular flap. Press the folds flat.

**8** This should be the result. Unfold the paper, bringing it into the position shown in the next step.

**9** Here is the completed connector.

Mama Panda © 2013 Katrin and Yuri Shumakov

# Assembly

Prepare all the elements: Mama Panda Head, Connector and Panda Body, the regular one or its tubby version.

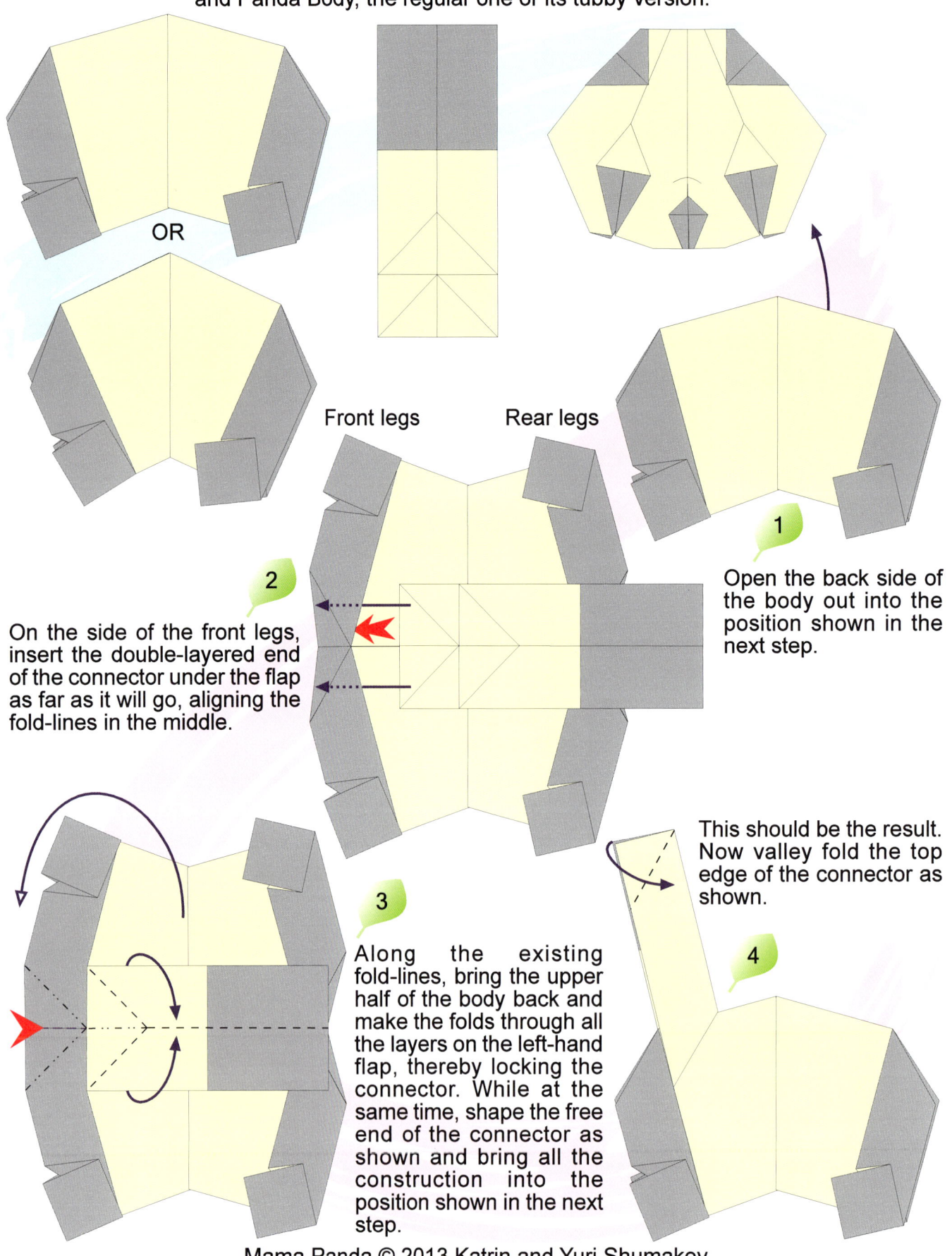

OR

Front legs    Rear legs

**1** Open the back side of the body out into the position shown in the next step.

**2** On the side of the front legs, insert the double-layered end of the connector under the flap as far as it will go, aligning the fold-lines in the middle.

**3** Along the existing fold-lines, bring the upper half of the body back and make the folds through all the layers on the left-hand flap, thereby locking the connector. While at the same time, shape the free end of the connector as shown and bring all the construction into the position shown in the next step.

This should be the result. Now valley fold the top edge of the connector as shown.

**4**

Mama Panda © 2013 Katrin and Yuri Shumakov

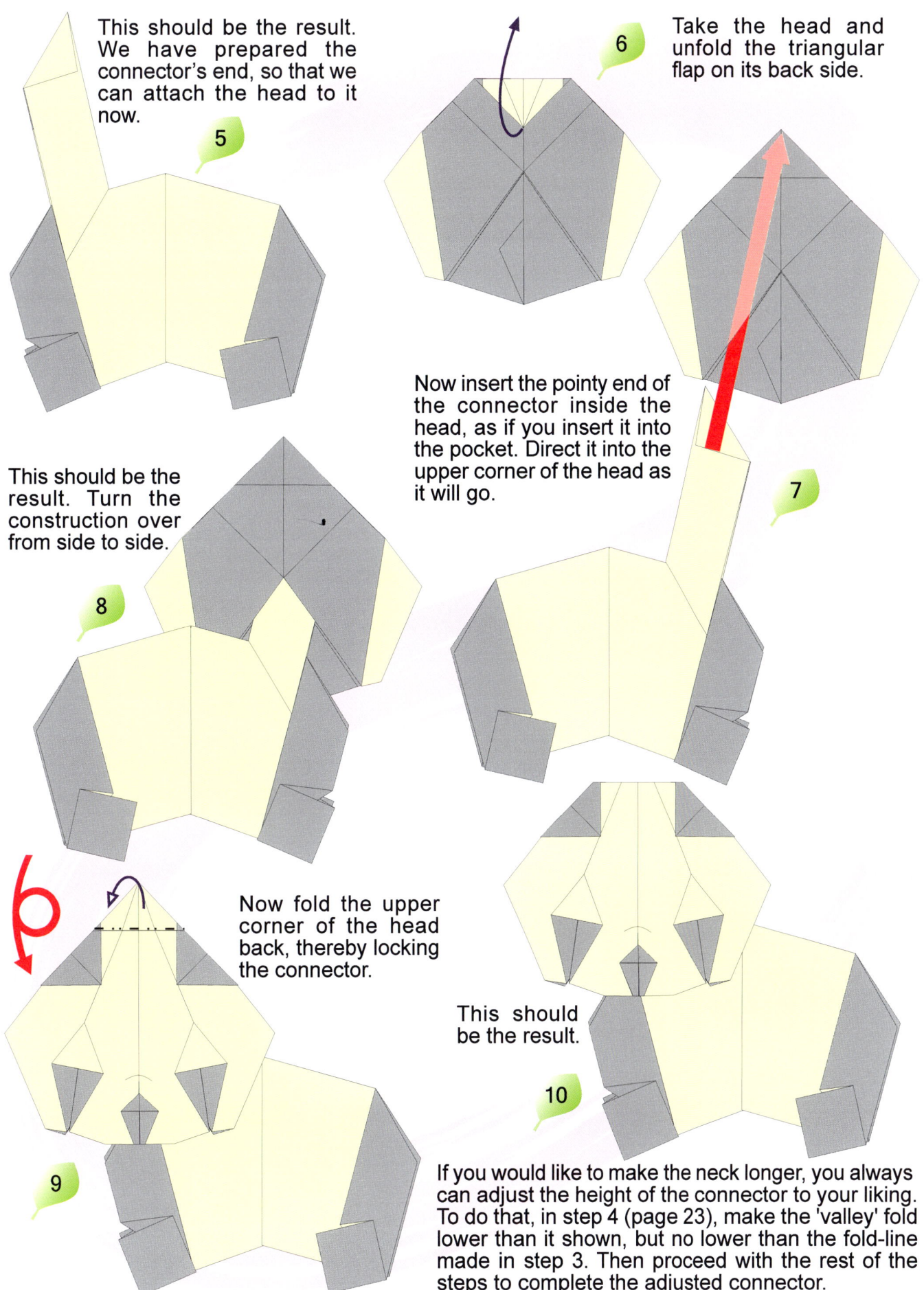

This should be the result. We have prepared the connector's end, so that we can attach the head to it now.

5

6 Take the head and unfold the triangular flap on its back side.

Now insert the pointy end of the connector inside the head, as if you insert it into the pocket. Direct it into the upper corner of the head as it will go.

7

This should be the result. Turn the construction over from side to side.

8

Now fold the upper corner of the head back, thereby locking the connector.

This should be the result.

10

9

If you would like to make the neck longer, you always can adjust the height of the connector to your liking. To do that, in step 4 (page 23), make the 'valley' fold lower than it shown, but no lower than the fold-line made in step 3. Then proceed with the rest of the steps to complete the adjusted connector.

Mama Panda © 2013 Katrin and Yuri Shumakov

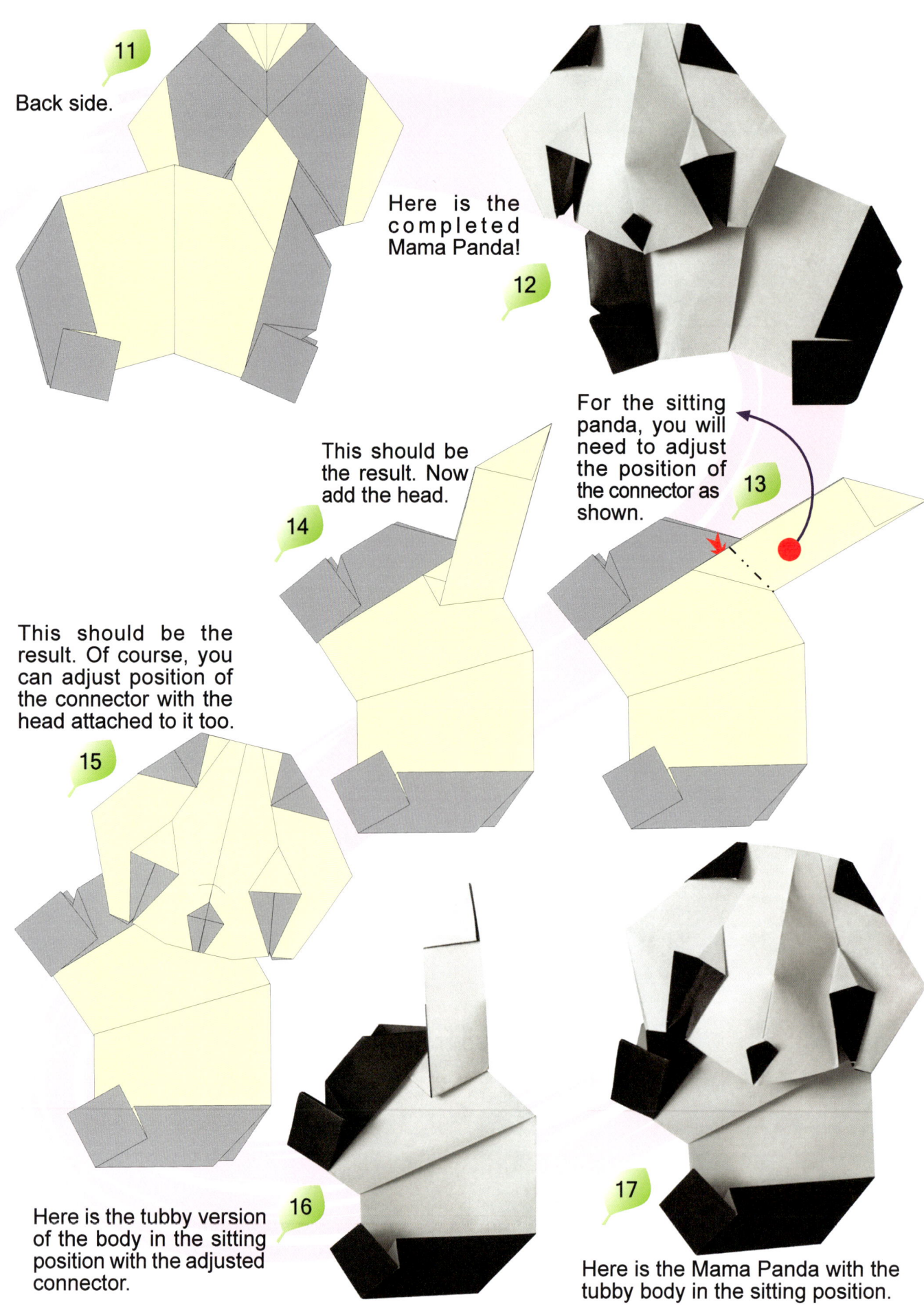

**11** Back side.

**12** Here is the completed Mama Panda!

For the sitting panda, you will need to adjust the position of the connector as shown. **13**

**14** This should be the result. Now add the head.

This should be the result. Of course, you can adjust position of the connector with the head attached to it too. **15**

Here is the tubby version of the body in the sitting position with the adjusted connector. **16**

Here is the Mama Panda with the tubby body in the sitting position. **17**

Mama Panda © 2013 Katrin and Yuri Shumakov

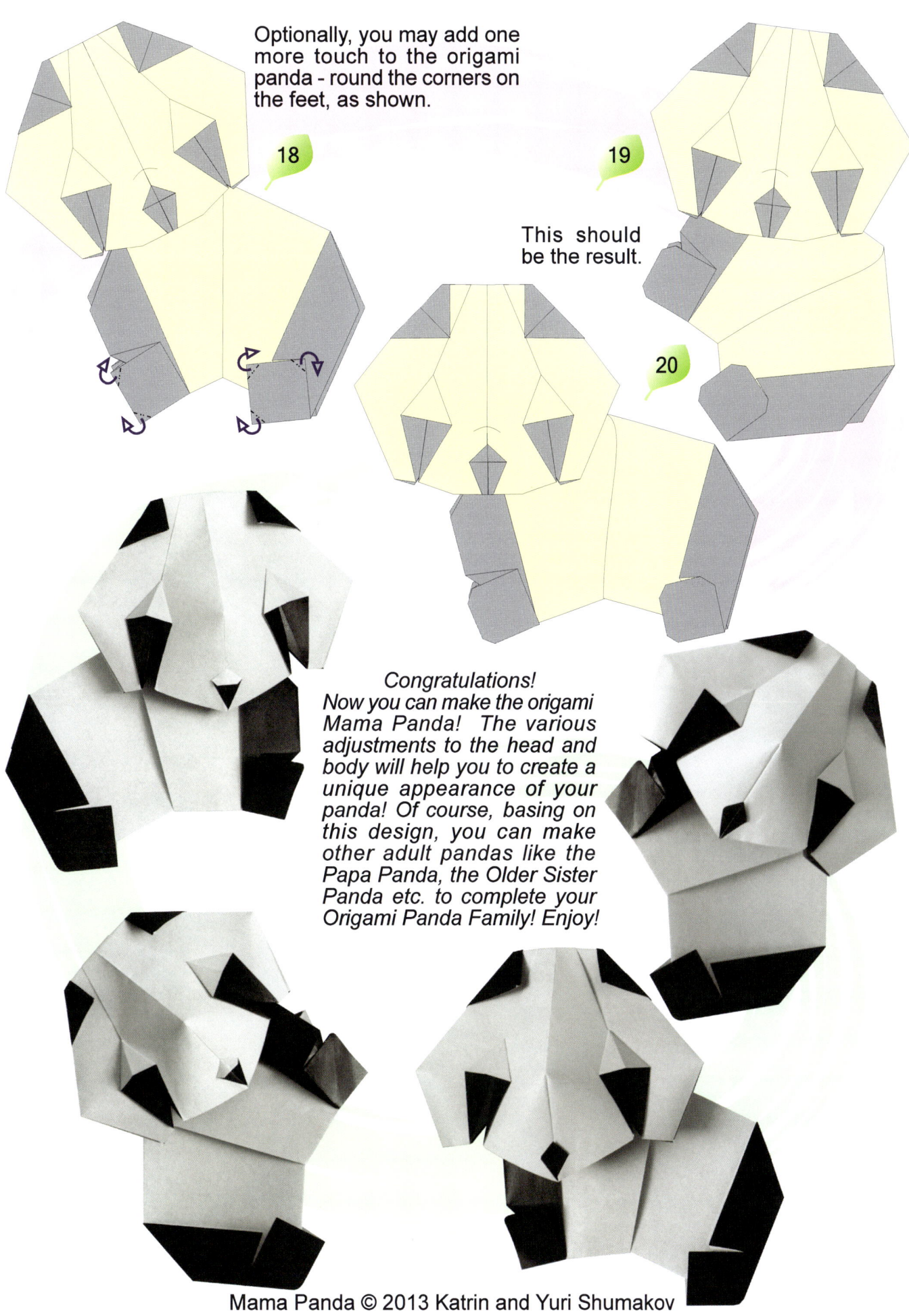

Optionally, you may add one more touch to the origami panda - round the corners on the feet, as shown.

18

19

This should be the result.

20

Congratulations! Now you can make the origami *Mama Panda!* The various adjustments to the head and body will help you to create a unique appearance of your panda! Of course, basing on this design, you can make other adult pandas like the *Papa Panda*, the *Older Sister Panda* etc. to complete your Origami Panda Family! Enjoy!

Mama Panda © 2013 Katrin and Yuri Shumakov

# Baby Panda
## by Yuri & Katrin Shumakov

This adorable Baby Panda design folds from 2 squares used for the head and the body. A strip, 1:4 in proportion, will be needed to connect two parts together with paper locks without any glue. Variations of the panda body can be used with this design to make the older Panda kids and the younger ones. You will be able to adjust the position of the body and the head to your liking.

**Suggested paper:** Regular origami paper.

**Suggested sizes:** Use two 6-inch (15 cm) squares and a strip 1-1/2x6 inches (3.75x15cm). Or two 5-inch (12.5 cm) squares and a strip 1-1/4x5 inches (3x12.5cm). When you master the model, you can use smaller paper like 3-inch (7.5cm) squares.

**Suggested colors:** It's natural to use two-color paper in black and white.

The finished model will fit into an original square, used for folding, with some spare space, as pictured.

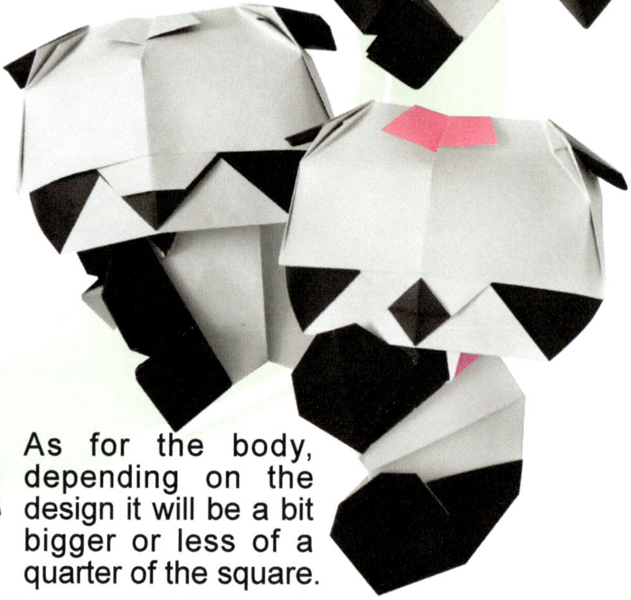

The head will be about 2/3 of the side of the square long and about a half of the side of the square high.

As for the body, depending on the design it will be a bit bigger or less of a quarter of the square.

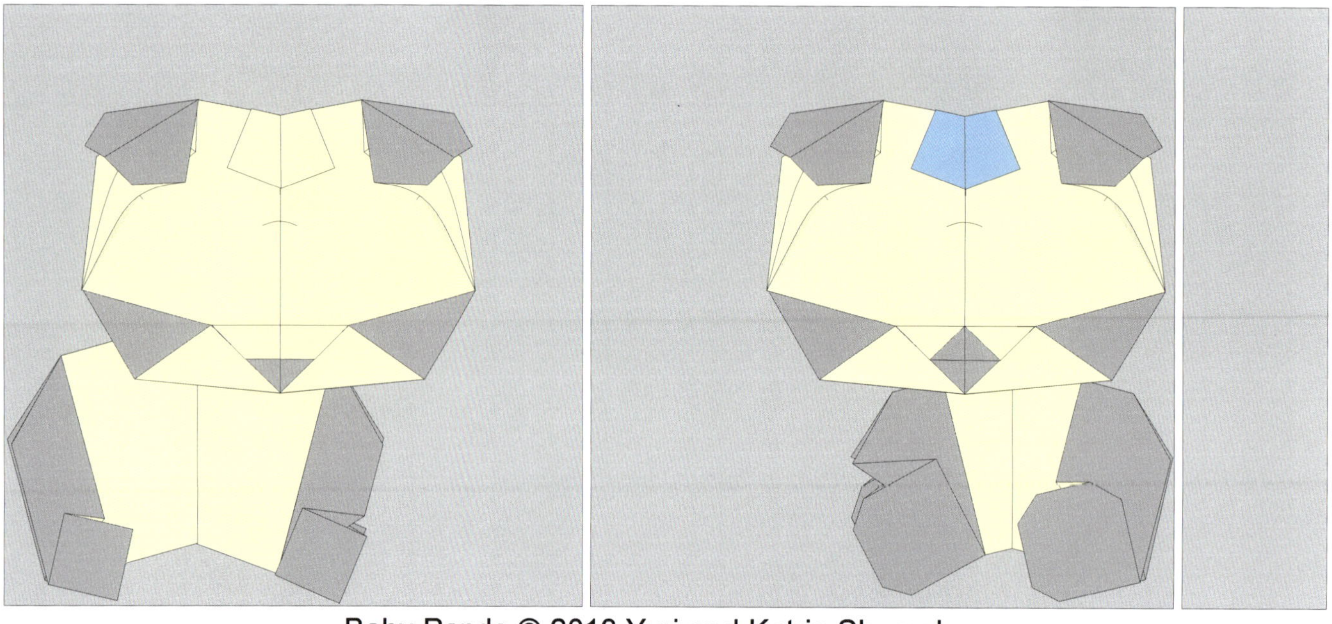

Baby Panda © 2013 Yuri and Katrin Shumakov

# Baby Panda Head

Take a square of paper.

*Begin with colored side up.*

Valley fold the square in half from corner to corner in turn to mark the diagonal fold line. Press it flat and unfold it.

**1**

Valley fold the square in half from top to bottom.

**2**

Separate the front layer and valley fold it up in half, as shown.

**3**

Unfold the middle triangular flap down.

**5**

Now valley fold the side points to meet the middle of the top edge.

**4**

Working with one of the square flaps, valley fold the lower sloping edges to the middle fold-line. Repeat with the other flap.

**8**

Working successively with each triangular flap, separate the layers, bringing one of the layers aside, and squash the flap into a square as shown in the next step.

**6**

On each of the resulted squares, separate the front layer and valley fold the bottom point up.

**7**

Baby Panda © 2013 Yuri and Katrin Shumakov

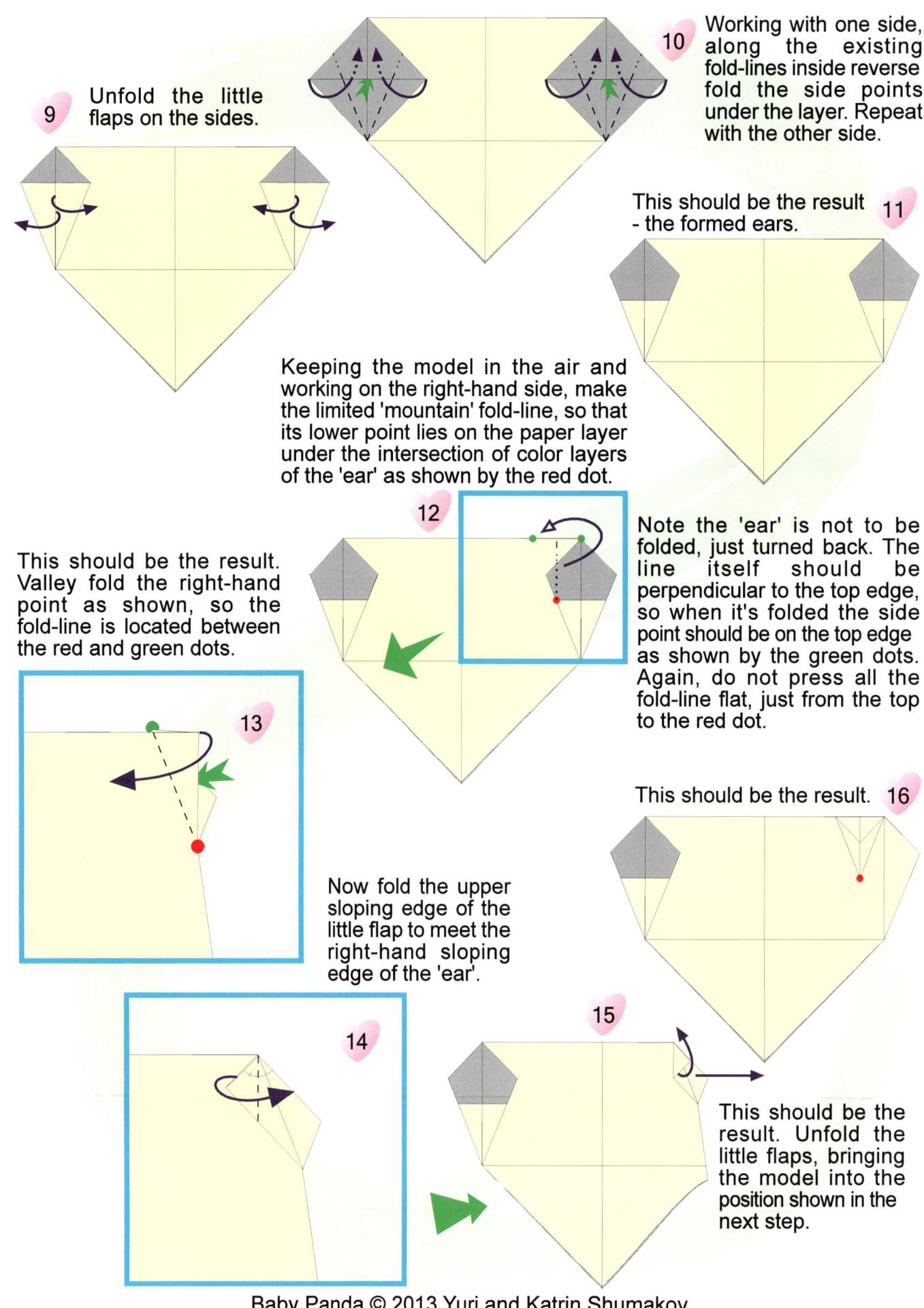

**9** Unfold the little flaps on the sides.

**10** Working with one side, along the existing fold-lines inside reverse fold the side points under the layer. Repeat with the other side.

**11** This should be the result - the formed ears.

Keeping the model in the air and working on the right-hand side, make the limited 'mountain' fold-line, so that its lower point lies on the paper layer under the intersection of color layers of the 'ear' as shown by the red dot.

**12**

Note the 'ear' is not to be folded, just turned back. The line itself should be perpendicular to the top edge, so when it's folded the side point should be on the top edge as shown by the green dots. Again, do not press all the fold-line flat, just from the top to the red dot.

**13** This should be the result. Valley fold the right-hand point as shown, so the fold-line is located between the red and green dots.

**16** This should be the result.

Now fold the upper sloping edge of the little flap to meet the right-hand sloping edge of the 'ear'.

**14**

**15** This should be the result. Unfold the little flaps, bringing the model into the position shown in the next step.

Baby Panda © 2013 Yuri and Katrin Shumakov

Now we'll repeat steps 12-15 as in mirror for the left-hand side. Make the limited 'mountain' fold-line, as shown. Note the 'ear' is not to be folded, just turned back.

17

18

Valley fold the left-hand point as shown, so the fold-line is located between the red and green dots.

Fold the upper sloping edge of the little flap to meet the left-hand sloping edge of the 'ear'.

19

Unfold the little flaps, bringing the model into the position shown in the next step.

20

Now mountain fold the right-hand half of the model as shown.

21

This should be the result. Turn the 'ear' parts toward you.

24

Valley fold the upper right-hand corner as shown, so that the fold-line is parallel to the line, marked in blue, and starts at the same level (shown by the dotted line).

22

23

This should be the result. Now unfold the resulted flap and bring the back half of the model to the right.

Baby Panda © 2013 Yuri and Katrin Shumakov

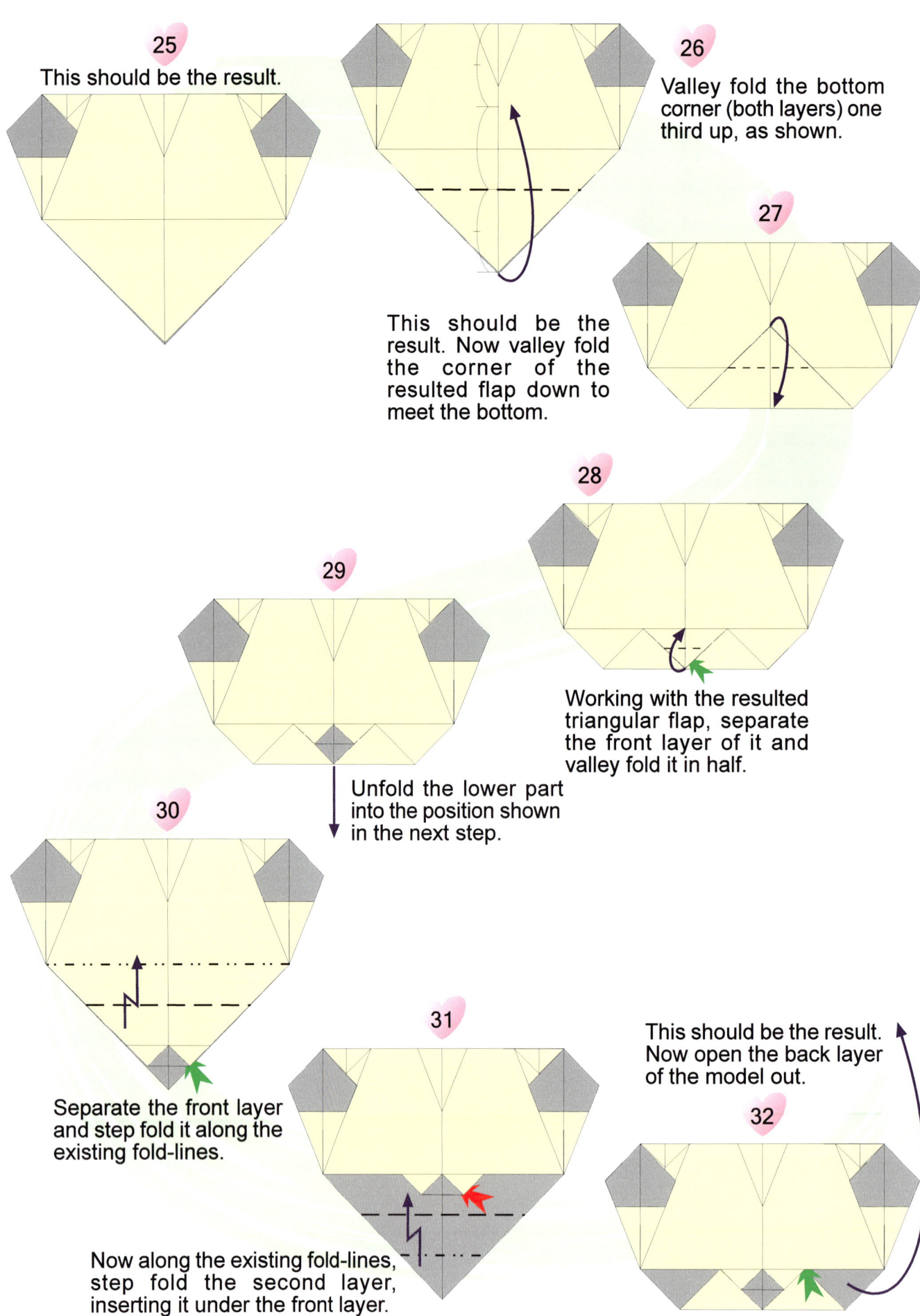

**25**
This should be the result.

**26**
Valley fold the bottom corner (both layers) one third up, as shown.

This should be the result. Now valley fold the corner of the resulted flap down to meet the bottom.

**27**

**28**
Working with the resulted triangular flap, separate the front layer of it and valley fold it in half.

**29**
Unfold the lower part into the position shown in the next step.

**30**
Separate the front layer and step fold it along the existing fold-lines.

**31**
Now along the existing fold-lines, step fold the second layer, inserting it under the front layer.

This should be the result. Now open the back layer of the model out.

**32**

Baby Panda © 2013 Yuri and Katrin Shumakov

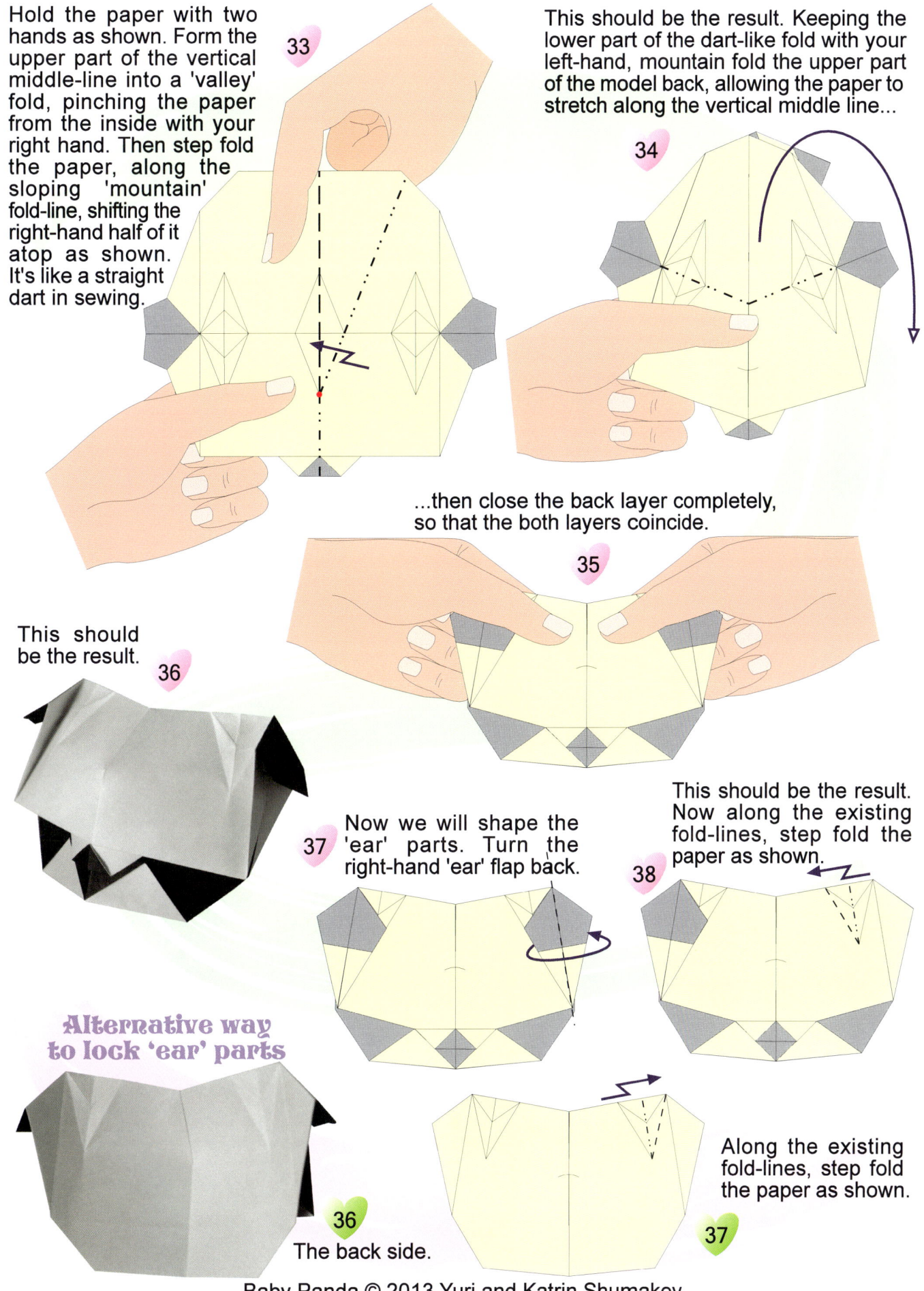

Hold the paper with two hands as shown. Form the upper part of the vertical middle-line into a 'valley' fold, pinching the paper from the inside with your right hand. Then step fold the paper, along the sloping 'mountain' fold-line, shifting the right-hand half of it atop as shown. It's like a straight dart in sewing.

**33**

This should be the result. Keeping the lower part of the dart-like fold with your left-hand, mountain fold the upper part of the model back, allowing the paper to stretch along the vertical middle line...

**34**

...then close the back layer completely, so that the both layers coincide.

**35**

This should be the result.

**36**

Now we will shape the 'ear' parts. Turn the right-hand 'ear' flap back.

**37**

This should be the result. Now along the existing fold-lines, step fold the paper as shown.

**38**

*Alternative way to lock 'ear' parts*

**36**

The back side.

Along the existing fold-lines, step fold the paper as shown.

**37**

Baby Panda © 2013 Yuri and Katrin Shumakov

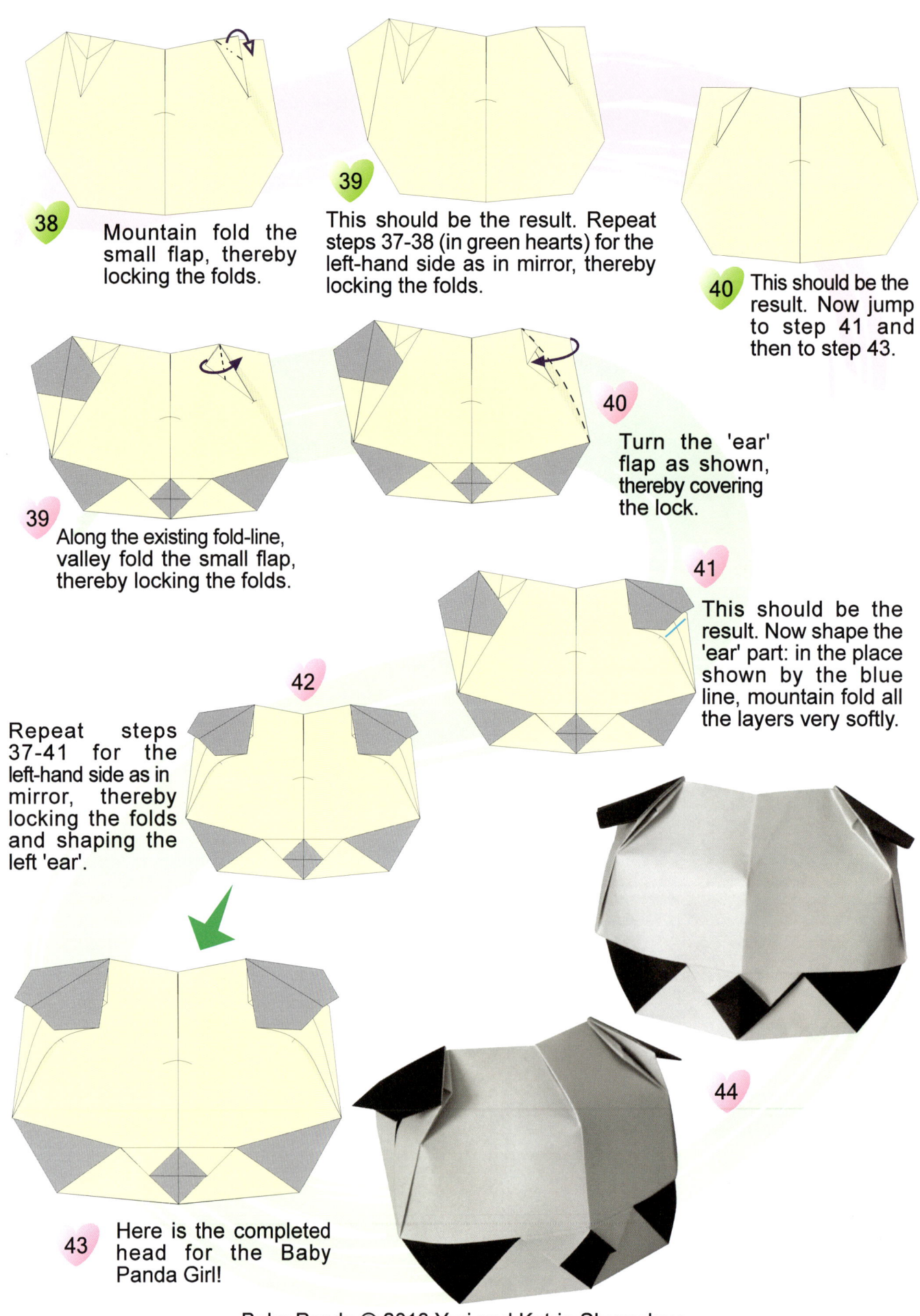

**38** Mountain fold the small flap, thereby locking the folds.

**39** This should be the result. Repeat steps 37-38 (in green hearts) for the left-hand side as in mirror, thereby locking the folds.

**40** This should be the result. Now jump to step 41 and then to step 43.

**39** Along the existing fold-line, valley fold the small flap, thereby locking the folds.

**40** Turn the 'ear' flap as shown, thereby covering the lock.

**41** This should be the result. Now shape the 'ear' part: in the place shown by the blue line, mountain fold all the layers very softly.

**42** Repeat steps 37-41 for the left-hand side as in mirror, thereby locking the folds and shaping the left 'ear'.

**43** Here is the completed head for the Baby Panda Girl!

**44**

Baby Panda © 2013 Yuri and Katrin Shumakov

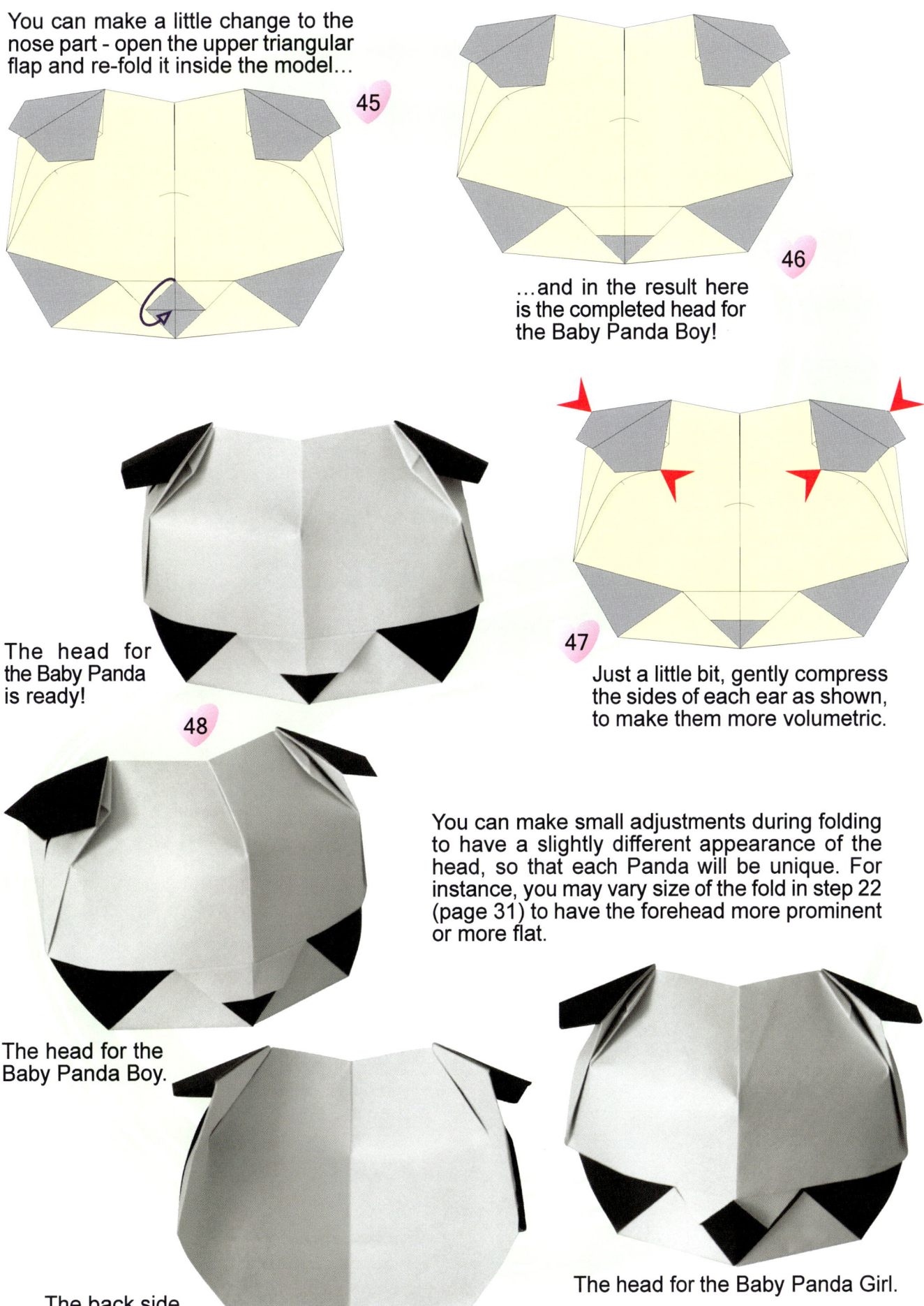

You can make a little change to the nose part - open the upper triangular flap and re-fold it inside the model…

45

46

…and in the result here is the completed head for the Baby Panda Boy!

The head for the Baby Panda is ready!

47

Just a little bit, gently compress the sides of each ear as shown, to make them more volumetric.

48

The head for the Baby Panda Boy.

You can make small adjustments during folding to have a slightly different appearance of the head, so that each Panda will be unique. For instance, you may vary size of the fold in step 22 (page 31) to have the forehead more prominent or more flat.

The back side.

The head for the Baby Panda Girl.

Baby Panda © 2013 Yuri and Katrin Shumakov

# Baby Panda Body

While you already may use the Panda Body and Panda Tubby Body (pages 16-22) with the Baby Panda Head to make older Panda kids, here is how to make the Baby Panda Body for the younger Panda kids.

Take a square identical in size to the paper square used for the head.

*Begin with colored side up.*

Valley fold the opposite sides together in both directions, and open them up. Then turn the paper over.

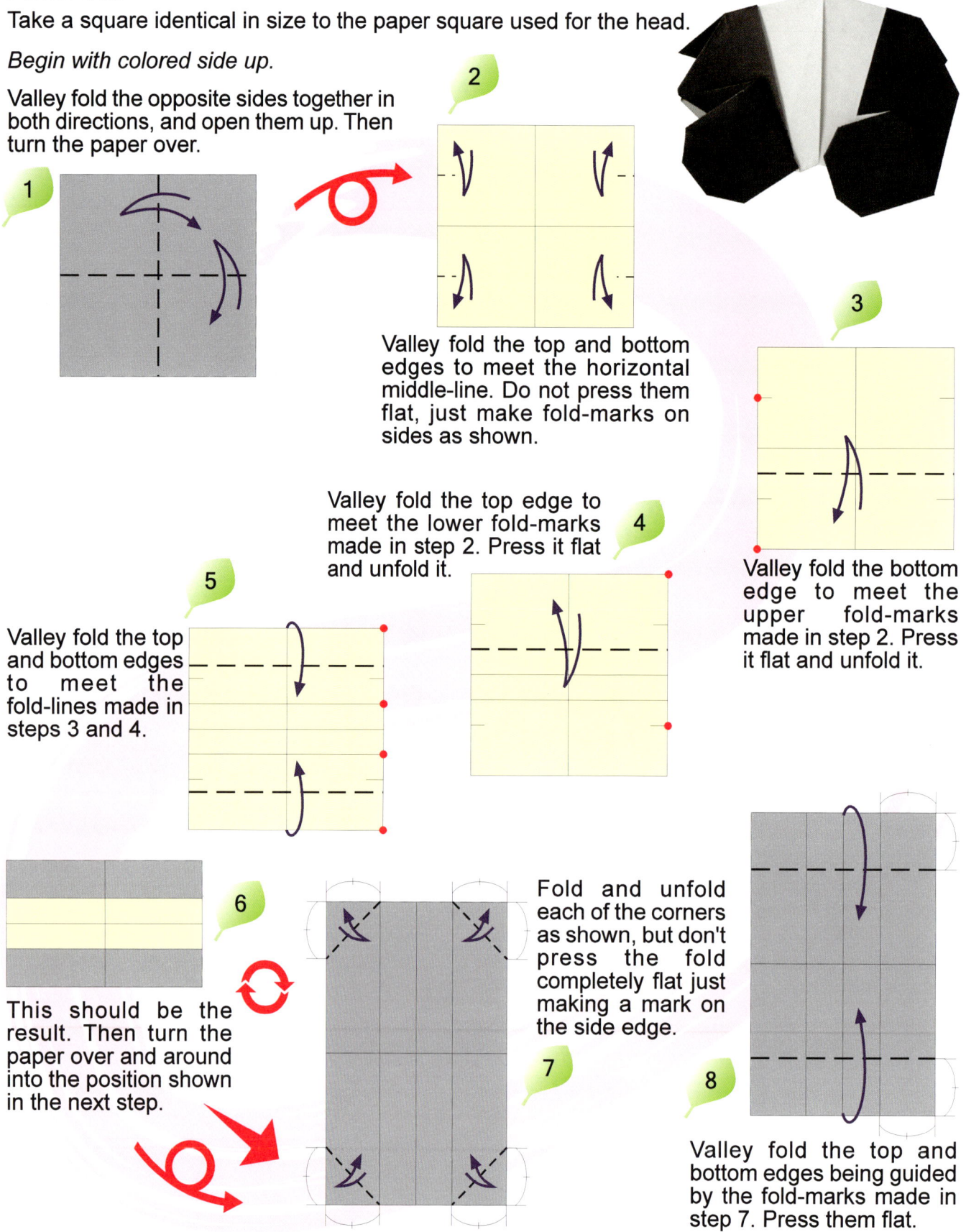

Valley fold the top and bottom edges to meet the horizontal middle-line. Do not press them flat, just make fold-marks on sides as shown.

Valley fold the top edge to meet the lower fold-marks made in step 2. Press it flat and unfold it.

Valley fold the bottom edge to meet the upper fold-marks made in step 2. Press it flat and unfold it.

Valley fold the top and bottom edges to meet the fold-lines made in steps 3 and 4.

This should be the result. Then turn the paper over and around into the position shown in the next step.

Fold and unfold each of the corners as shown, but don't press the fold completely flat just making a mark on the side edge.

Valley fold the top and bottom edges being guided by the fold-marks made in step 7. Press them flat.

Baby Panda © 2013 Yuri and Katrin Shumakov

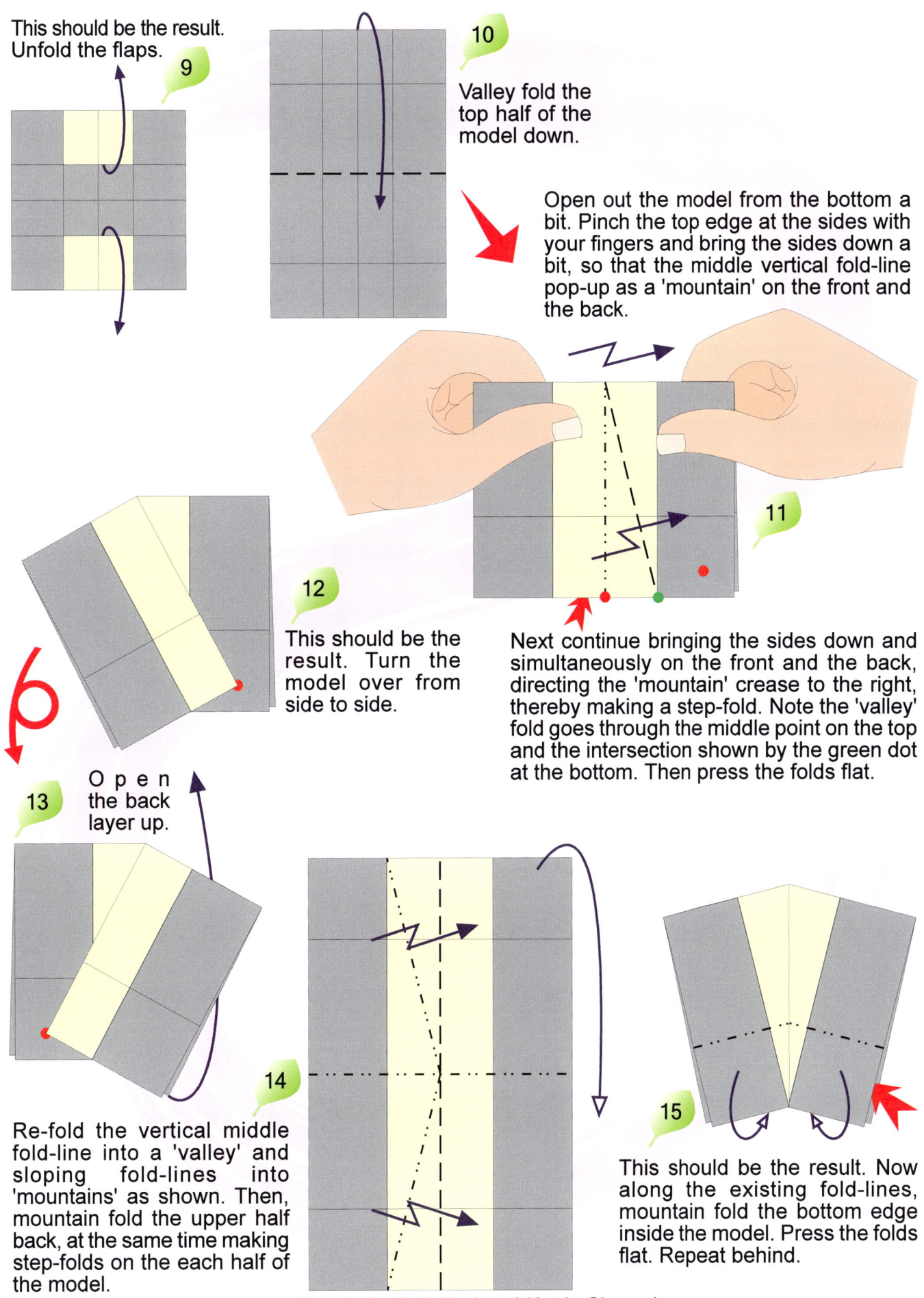

This should be the result. Unfold the flaps.

9

10

Valley fold the top half of the model down.

Open out the model from the bottom a bit. Pinch the top edge at the sides with your fingers and bring the sides down a bit, so that the middle vertical fold-line pop-up as a 'mountain' on the front and the back.

11

12

This should be the result. Turn the model over from side to side.

Next continue bringing the sides down and simultaneously on the front and the back, directing the 'mountain' crease to the right, thereby making a step-fold. Note the 'valley' fold goes through the middle point on the top and the intersection shown by the green dot at the bottom. Then press the folds flat.

13

Open the back layer up.

14

Re-fold the vertical middle fold-line into a 'valley' and sloping fold-lines into 'mountains' as shown. Then, mountain fold the upper half back, at the same time making step-folds on the each half of the model.

15

This should be the result. Now along the existing fold-lines, mountain fold the bottom edge inside the model. Press the folds flat. Repeat behind.

Baby Panda © 2013 Yuri and Katrin Shumakov

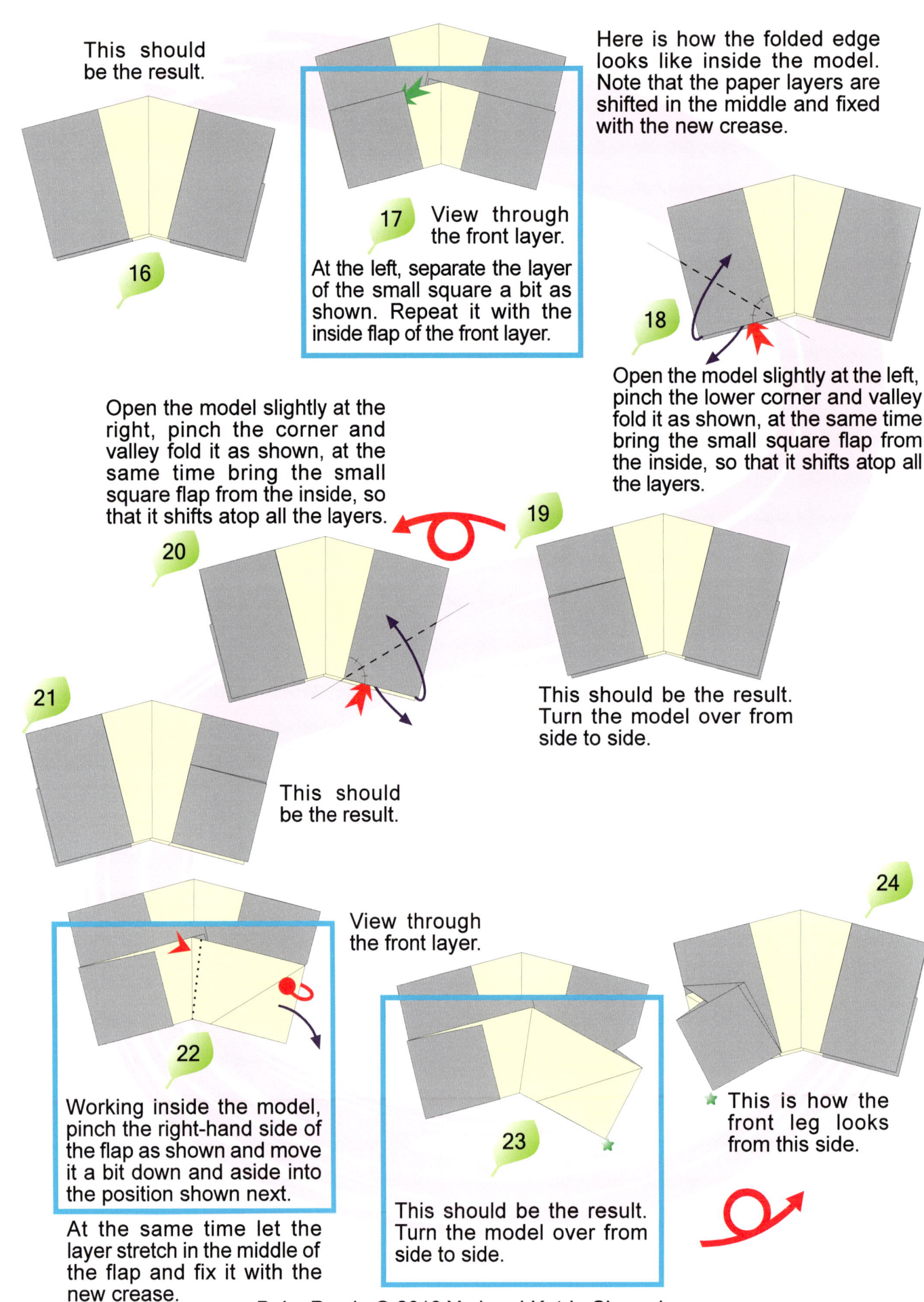

This should be the result.

16

17 View through the front layer.

At the left, separate the layer of the small square a bit as shown. Repeat it with the inside flap of the front layer.

Here is how the folded edge looks like inside the model. Note that the paper layers are shifted in the middle and fixed with the new crease.

18

Open the model slightly at the left, pinch the lower corner and valley fold it as shown, at the same time bring the small square flap from the inside, so that it shifts atop all the layers.

19

This should be the result. Turn the model over from side to side.

Open the model slightly at the right, pinch the corner and valley fold it as shown, at the same time bring the small square flap from the inside, so that it shifts atop all the layers.

20

21

This should be the result.

22

Working inside the model, pinch the right-hand side of the flap as shown and move it a bit down and aside into the position shown next.

At the same time let the layer stretch in the middle of the flap and fix it with the new crease.

View through the front layer.

23

This should be the result. Turn the model over from side to side.

24

★ This is how the front leg looks from this side.

Baby Panda © 2013 Yuri and Katrin Shumakov

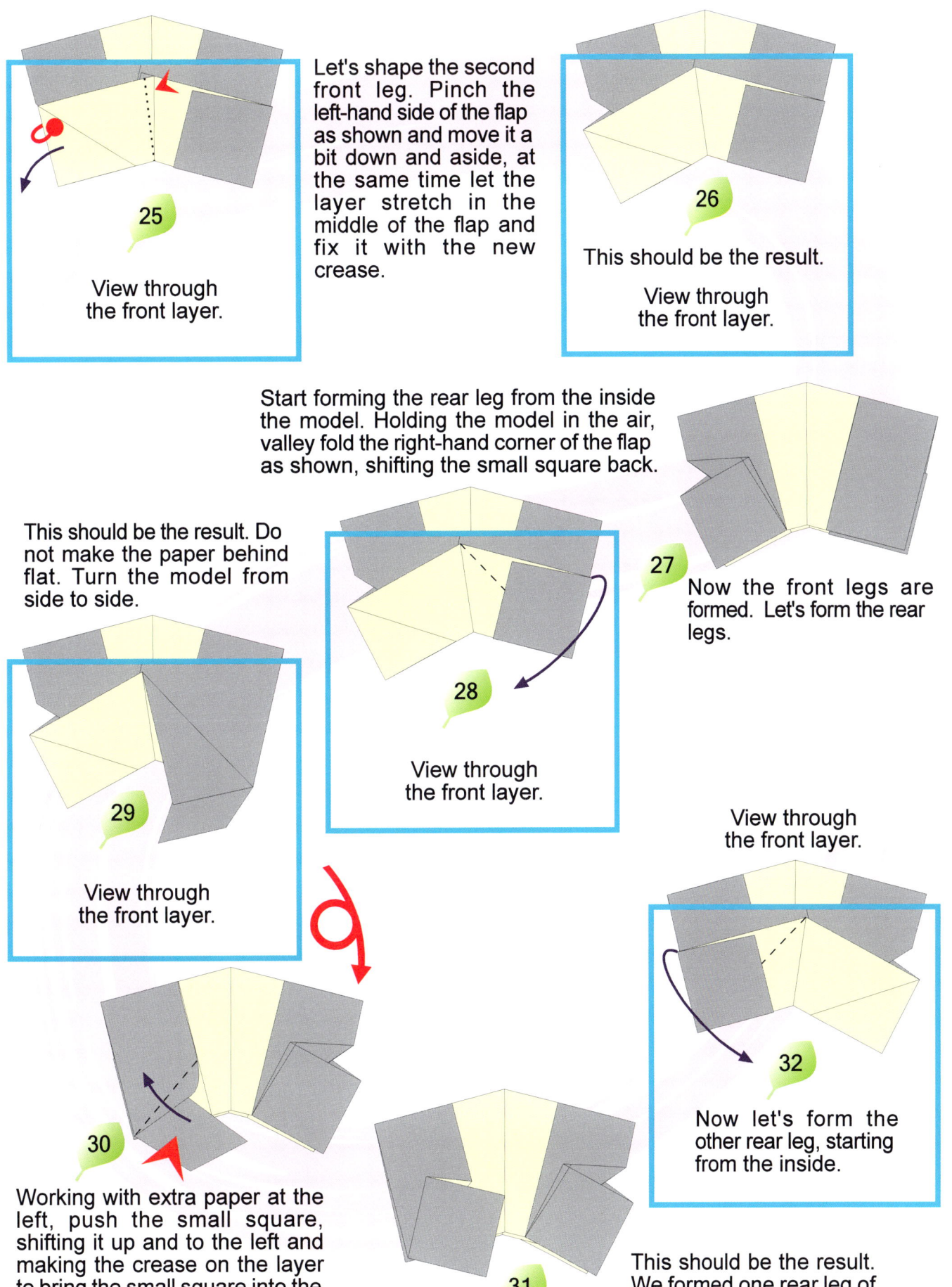

**25** View through the front layer.

Let's shape the second front leg. Pinch the left-hand side of the flap as shown and move it a bit down and aside, at the same time let the layer stretch in the middle of the flap and fix it with the new crease.

**26** This should be the result.
View through the front layer.

Start forming the rear leg from the inside the model. Holding the model in the air, valley fold the right-hand corner of the flap as shown, shifting the small square back.

**27** Now the front legs are formed. Let's form the rear legs.

This should be the result. Do not make the paper behind flat. Turn the model from side to side.

**28** View through the front layer.

**29** View through the front layer.

**30** Working with extra paper at the left, push the small square, shifting it up and to the left and making the crease on the layer to bring the small square into the position shown in the next step.

**31**

View through the front layer.

**32** Now let's form the other rear leg, starting from the inside.

This should be the result. We formed one rear leg of the panda body.

Baby Panda © 2013 Yuri and Katrin Shumakov

View through the front layer.

**33** This should be the result. Do not make the paper behind flat. Turn the model from side to side.

**34** Working with extra paper at the right, push the small square, shifting it up and to the right and making the crease on the layer to bring the small square into the position shown in the next step.

**35** Now working with all the layers, valley fold and unfold the upper side corners as shown.

**36** Along the fold-lines made in step 35, inside reverse fold the side points into the model, thereby rounding the body.

**37** Mountain fold the corners on the feet as shown, thereby shaping them more round.

The Baby Panda Body can be put in the sitting position.

**38** Front legs    Rear legs

**39** Here is the completed Baby Panda Body.

**40**

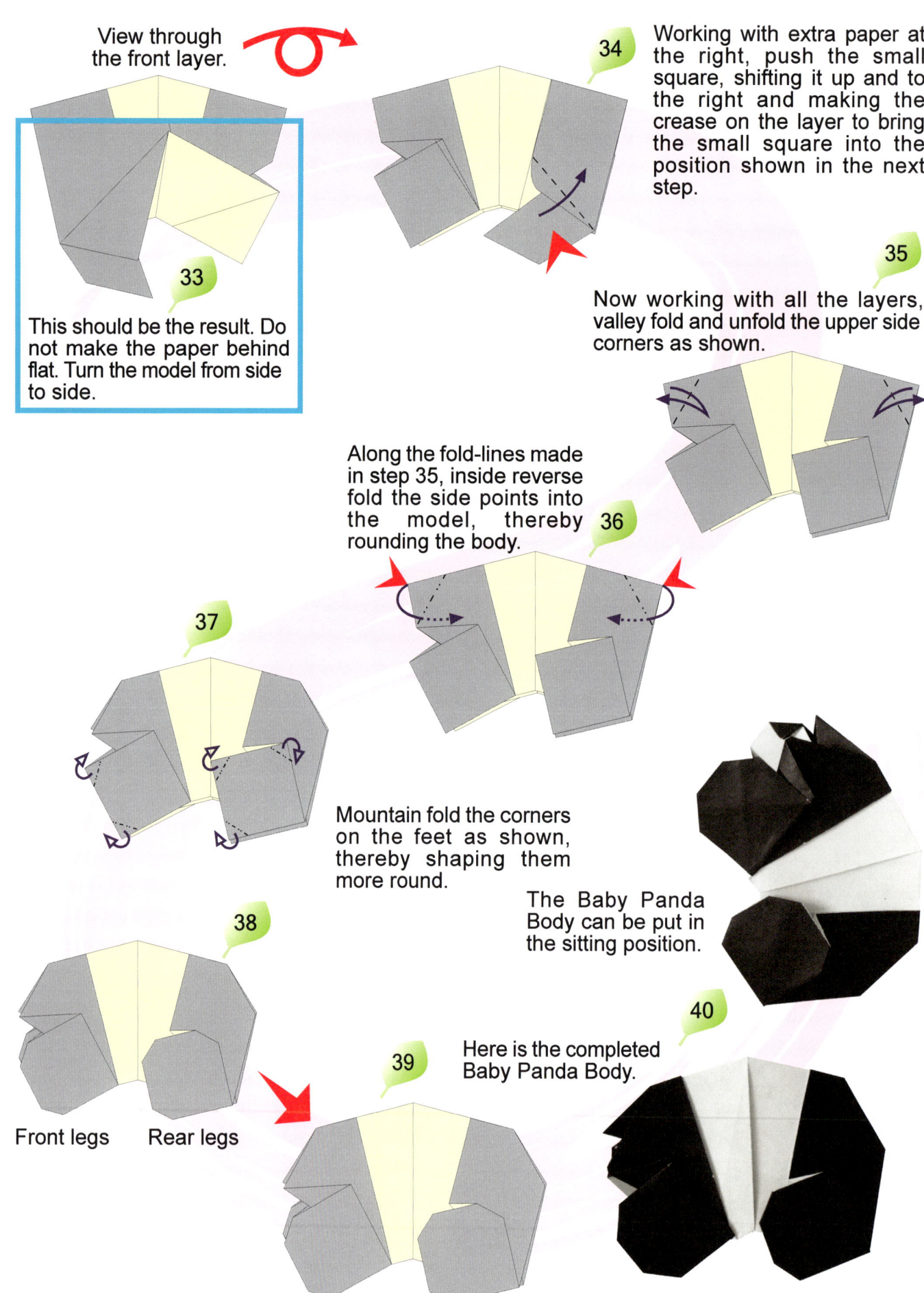

Baby Panda © 2013 Yuri and Katrin Shumakov

# Connector for Baby Panda Body

This connector will be used to unite the Baby Panda Head and Baby Panda Body together without any glue to make young Panda kids. Use a strip, 1:4 in proportion, which is 1/4 of the original square used to fold the head or body.

*Begin with colored side up.*

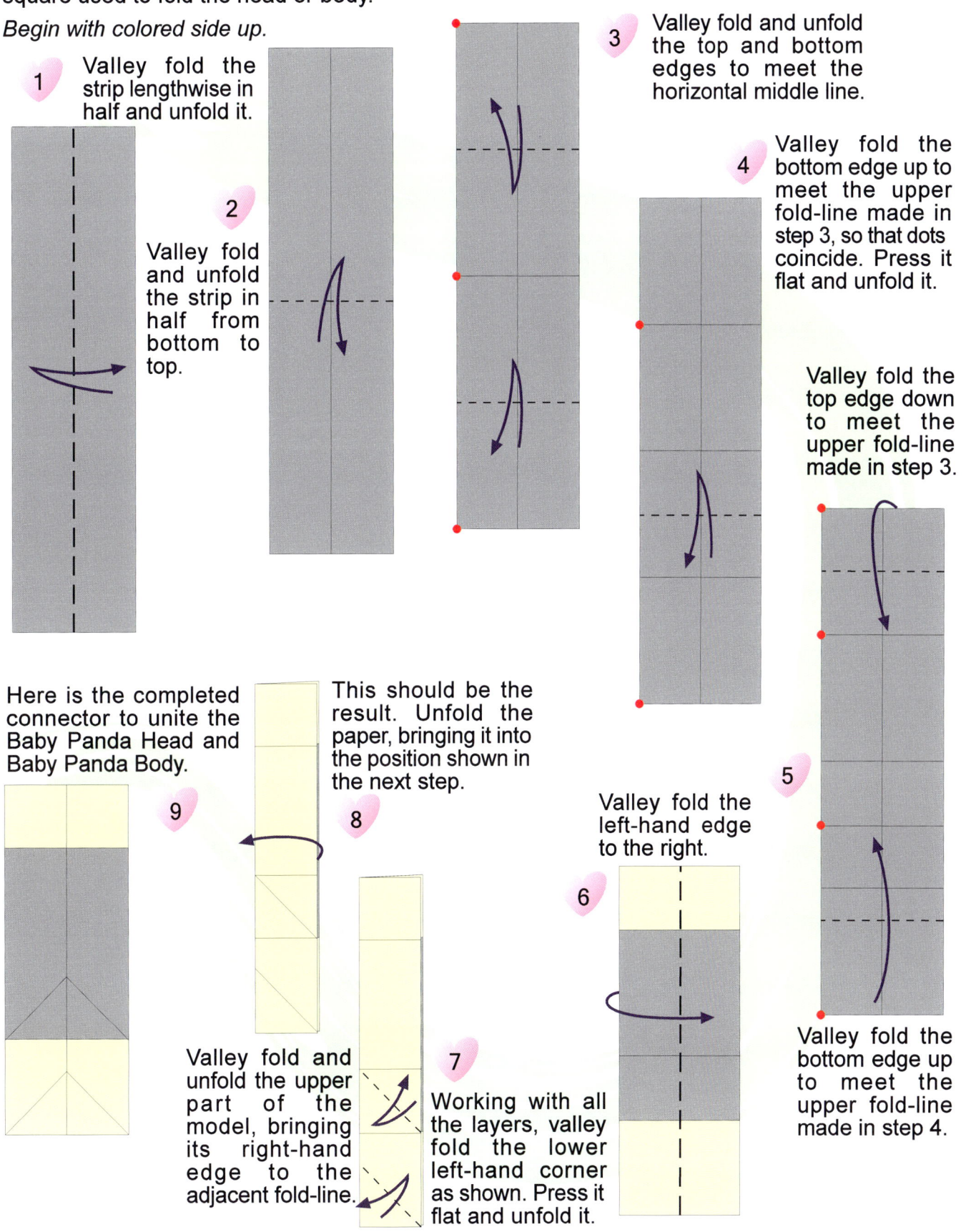

1 Valley fold the strip lengthwise in half and unfold it.

2 Valley fold and unfold the strip in half from bottom to top.

3 Valley fold and unfold the top and bottom edges to meet the horizontal middle line.

4 Valley fold the bottom edge up to meet the upper fold-line made in step 3, so that dots coincide. Press it flat and unfold it.

Valley fold the top edge down to meet the upper fold-line made in step 3.

5 Valley fold the bottom edge up to meet the upper fold-line made in step 4.

6 Valley fold the left-hand edge to the right.

7 Working with all the layers, valley fold the lower left-hand corner as shown. Press it flat and unfold it.

Valley fold and unfold the upper part of the model, bringing its right-hand edge to the adjacent fold-line.

8 This should be the result. Unfold the paper, bringing it into the position shown in the next step.

9 Here is the completed connector to unite the Baby Panda Head and Baby Panda Body.

Baby Panda © 2013 Yuri and Katrin Shumakov

# Connector for Panda Body & Tubby Body

This connector will be used to unite the Baby Panda Head and Panda Body or Panda Tubby Body (pages 16-22) together without any glue to make the older Panda kids. Use a strip, 1:4 in proportion, which is 1/4 of the original square used to fold the head or body.

*Begin with colored side up.*

Valley fold the strip lengthwise in half and unfold it.

**1**

**2** Valley fold and unfold the strip in half from bottom to top.

**3**

Valley fold the top and bottom edges to meet the horizontal middle line. Press them flat and unfold the upper part.

**4** Valley fold the top edge up to meet the upper fold-line made in step 3, so that dots coincide.

**5** Valley fold the left-hand edge to the right.

**6** Working with all the layers, valley fold the lower left-hand corner as shown. Press it flat.

**7** Valley fold the upper part of the model, bringing its right-hand edge to the upper edge of the small triangular flap. Press the folds flat.

**8** This should be the result. Unfold the paper, bringing it into the position shown in the next step.

**9** Here is the completed connector to unite the Baby Panda Head and Panda Body or Tubby Body.

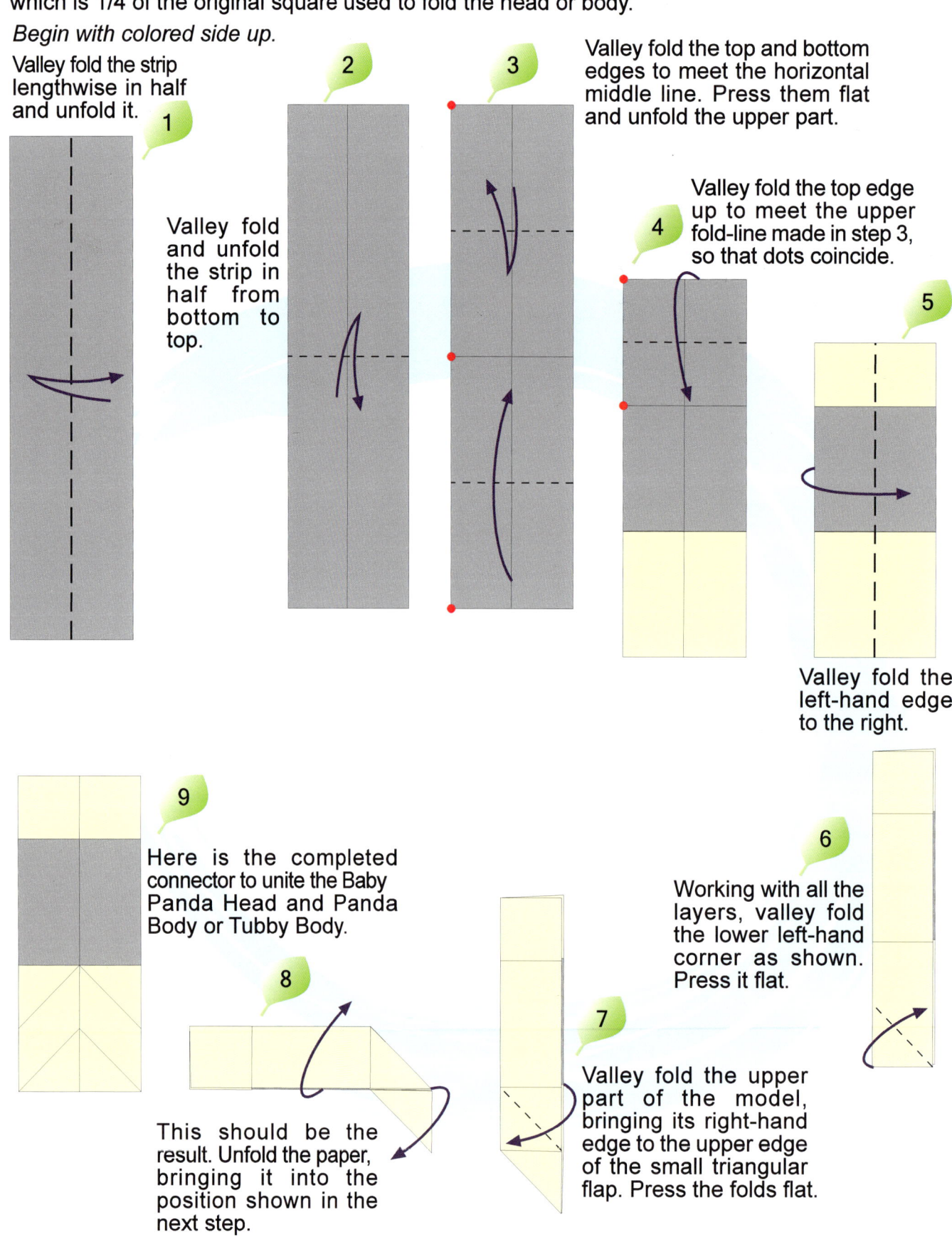

Baby Panda © 2013 Yuri and Katrin Shumakov

# Assembly

Prepare all the elements for your Baby Panda: Baby Panda Head, Connector and Panda Body, the regular one, its tubby version or the baby version.

Whatever type you have chosen to make, the assembly process is the same. The assembly is shown on an example of the first version with the Baby Panda Head, the regular Panda Body and its appropriate Connector.

## Baby Panda Head          Connector          Panda Body

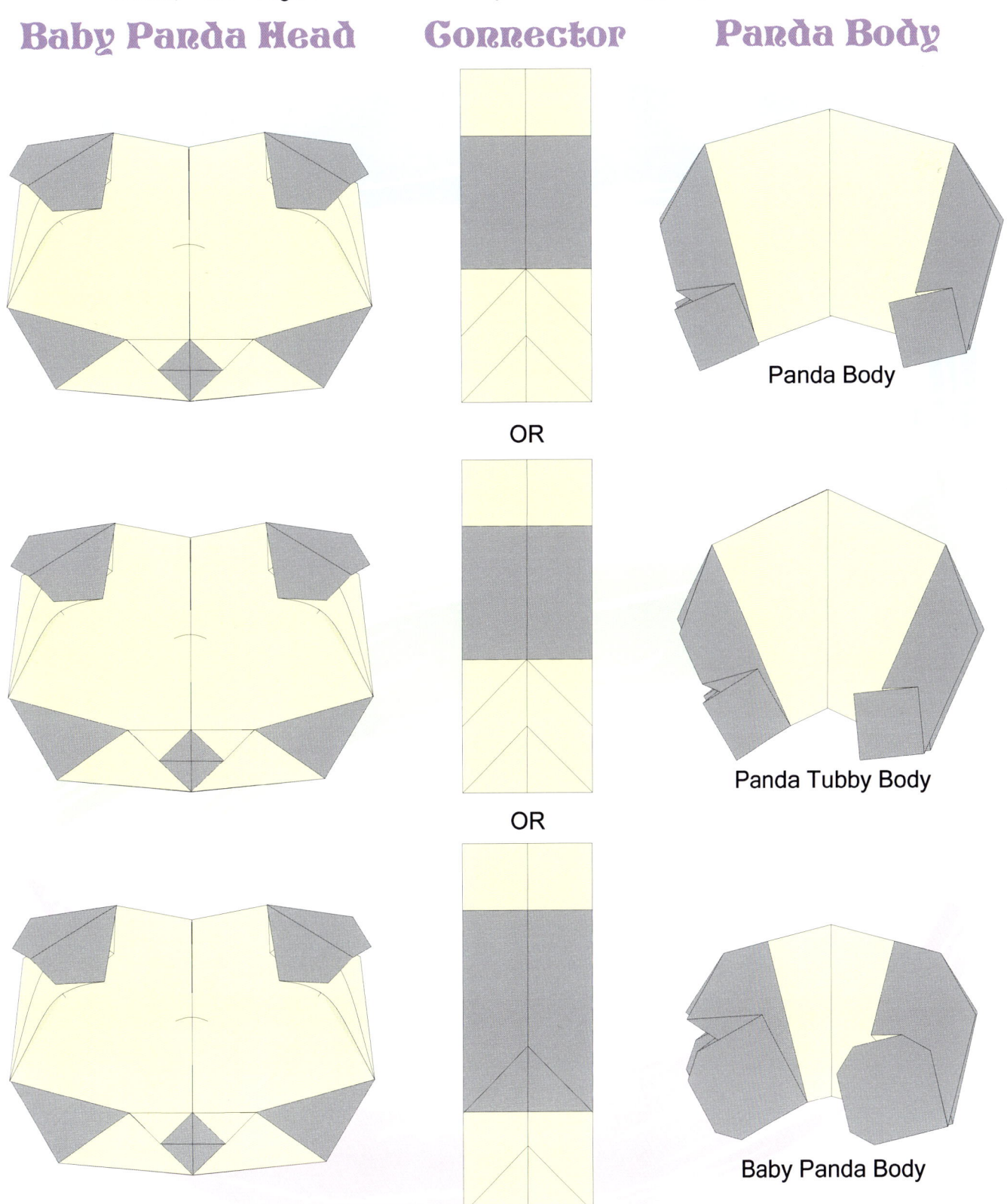

Panda Body

OR

Panda Tubby Body

OR

Baby Panda Body

Baby Panda © 2013 Yuri and Katrin Shumakov

# Uniting Baby Panda Head and Connector

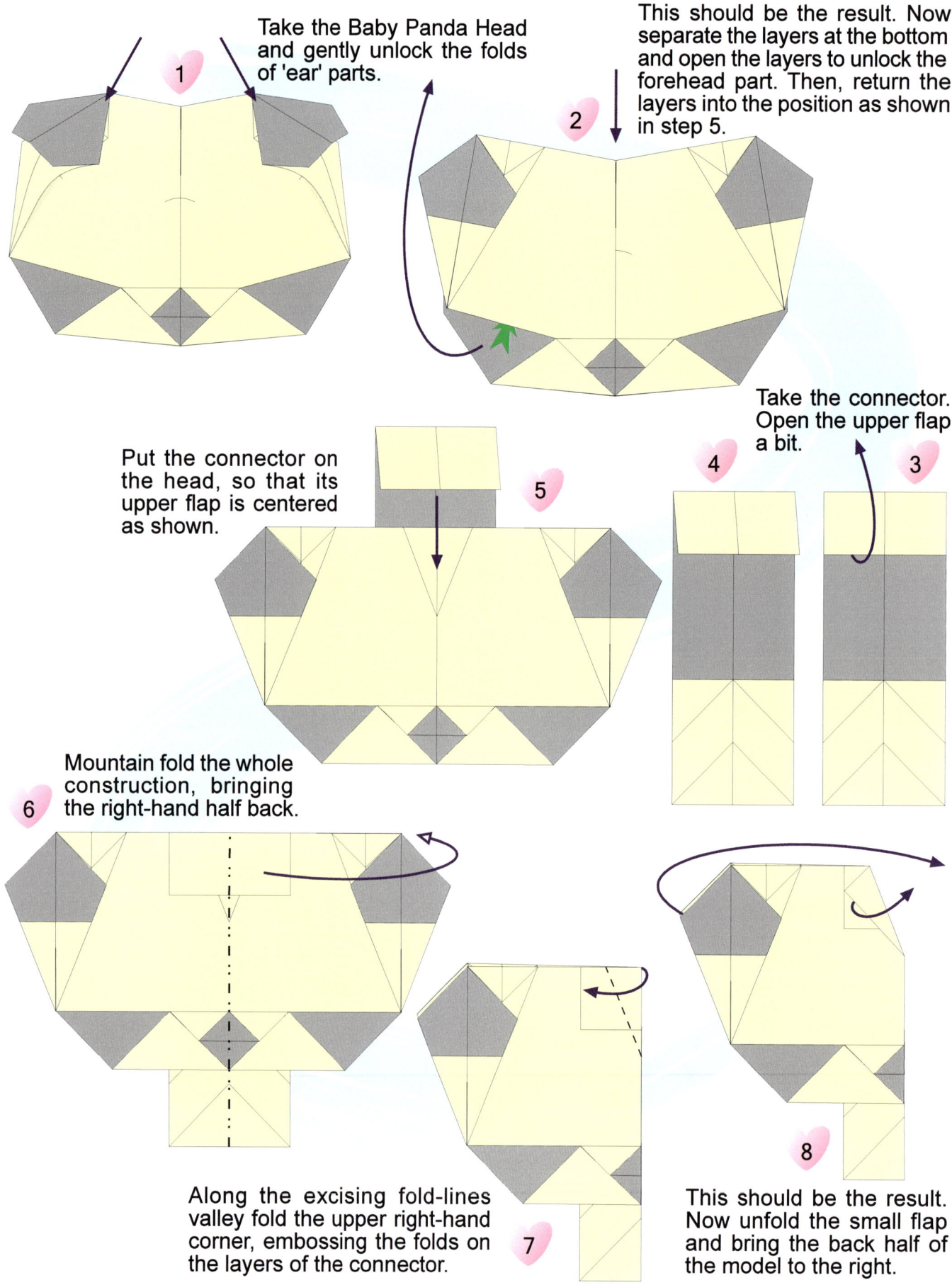

**1** Take the Baby Panda Head and gently unlock the folds of 'ear' parts.

**2** This should be the result. Now separate the layers at the bottom and open the layers to unlock the forehead part. Then, return the layers into the position as shown in step 5.

**3** Take the connector. Open the upper flap a bit.

**4**

**5** Put the connector on the head, so that its upper flap is centered as shown.

**6** Mountain fold the whole construction, bringing the right-hand half back.

**7** Along the excising fold-lines valley fold the upper right-hand corner, embossing the folds on the layers of the connector.

**8** This should be the result. Now unfold the small flap and bring the back half of the model to the right.

Baby Panda © 2013 Yuri and Katrin Shumakov

This should be the result. Now open the back layer of the model out, keeping the connector atop.

9

Now we will lock the head in the same way as shown in steps 33-35 on page 33, only with the connector atop. Before you start, be sure the connector aligned correctly.

10

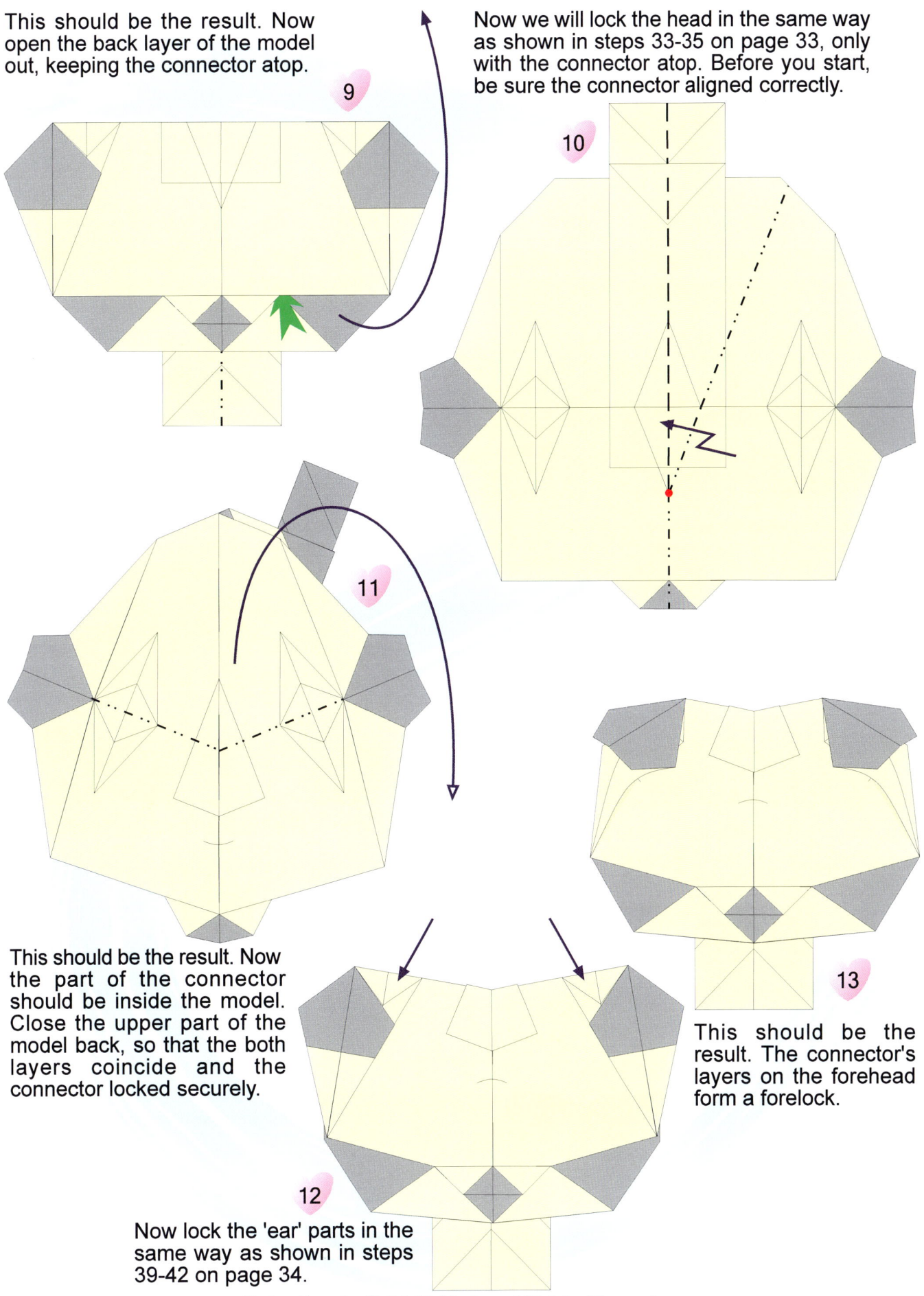

11

This should be the result. Now the part of the connector should be inside the model. Close the upper part of the model back, so that the both layers coincide and the connector locked securely.

12

Now lock the 'ear' parts in the same way as shown in steps 39-42 on page 34.

13

This should be the result. The connector's layers on the forehead form a forelock.

Baby Panda © 2013 Yuri and Katrin Shumakov

# Connecting Baby Panda Head and Body

14

The back side. The connector is securely locked.

15

Take the Panda Body as shown and open the back layer up.

Front legs          Rear legs

16

On the side of the front legs, insert the double-layered end of the connector under the flap as far as it will go, aligning the fold-lines in the middle.

These steps are similar to steps 2-4 on page 24.

17

Return the body into the initial position, thereby locking the connector in it. Bring the head up, making the creases on the connector.

The back side. Make the needed creases on the connector to secure the head position.

18

This should be the result.

19

Baby Panda © 2013 Yuri and Katrin Shumakov

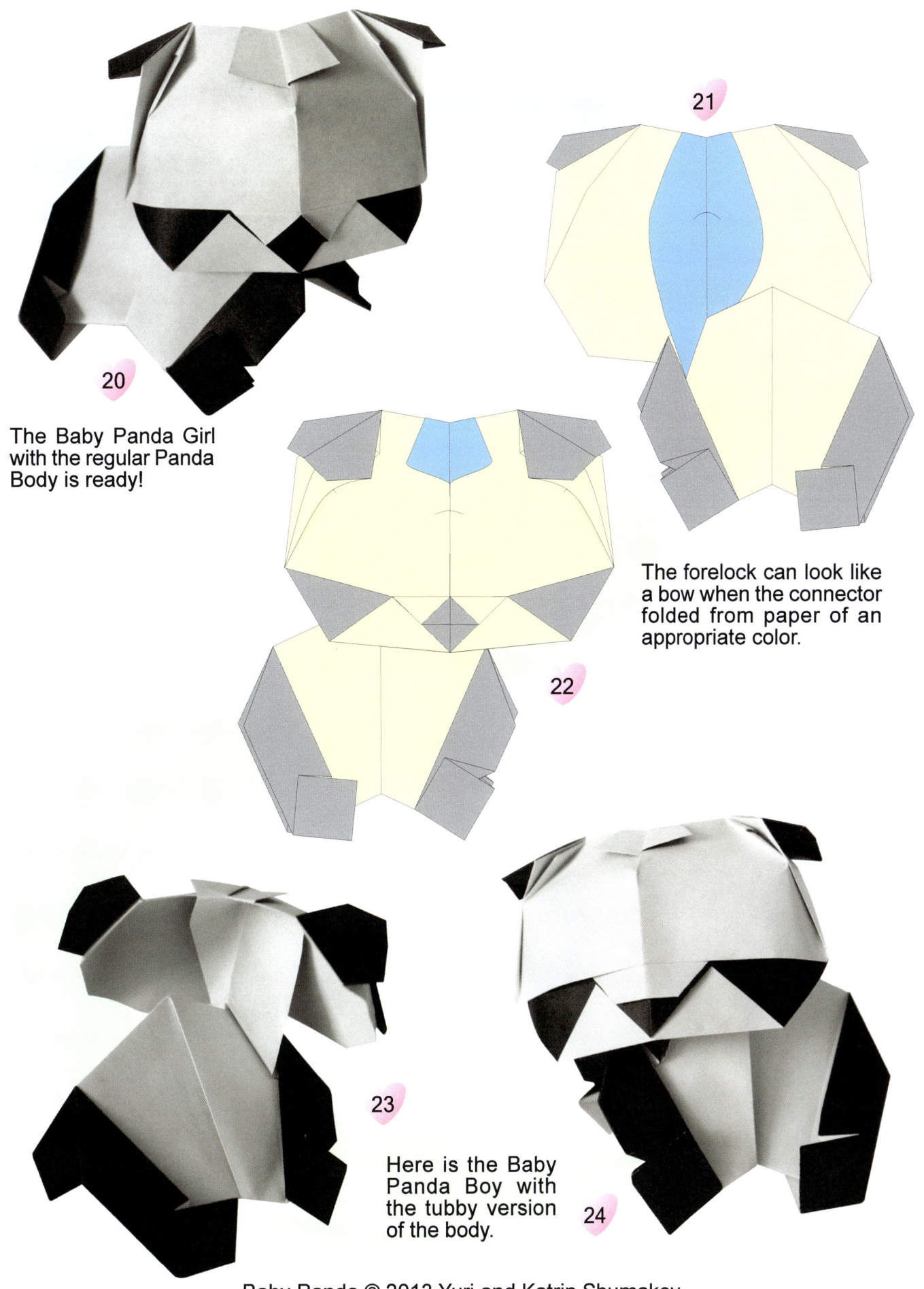

**20**

The Baby Panda Girl with the regular Panda Body is ready!

**21**

**22**

The forelock can look like a bow when the connector folded from paper of an appropriate color.

**23**

**24**

Here is the Baby Panda Boy with the tubby version of the body.

Baby Panda © 2013 Yuri and Katrin Shumakov

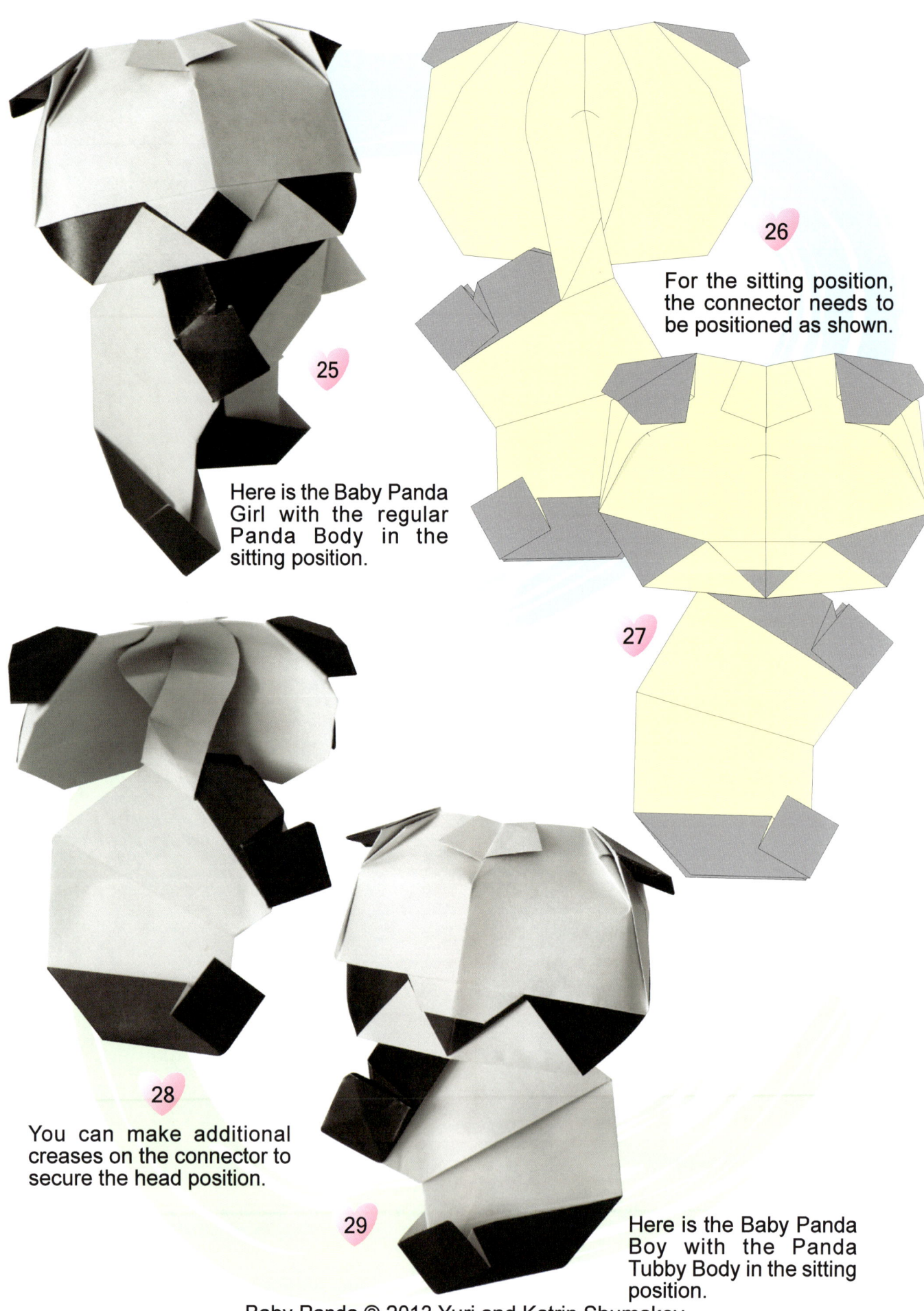

25

Here is the Baby Panda Girl with the regular Panda Body in the sitting position.

26

For the sitting position, the connector needs to be positioned as shown.

27

28

You can make additional creases on the connector to secure the head position.

29

Here is the Baby Panda Boy with the Panda Tubby Body in the sitting position.

Baby Panda © 2013 Yuri and Katrin Shumakov

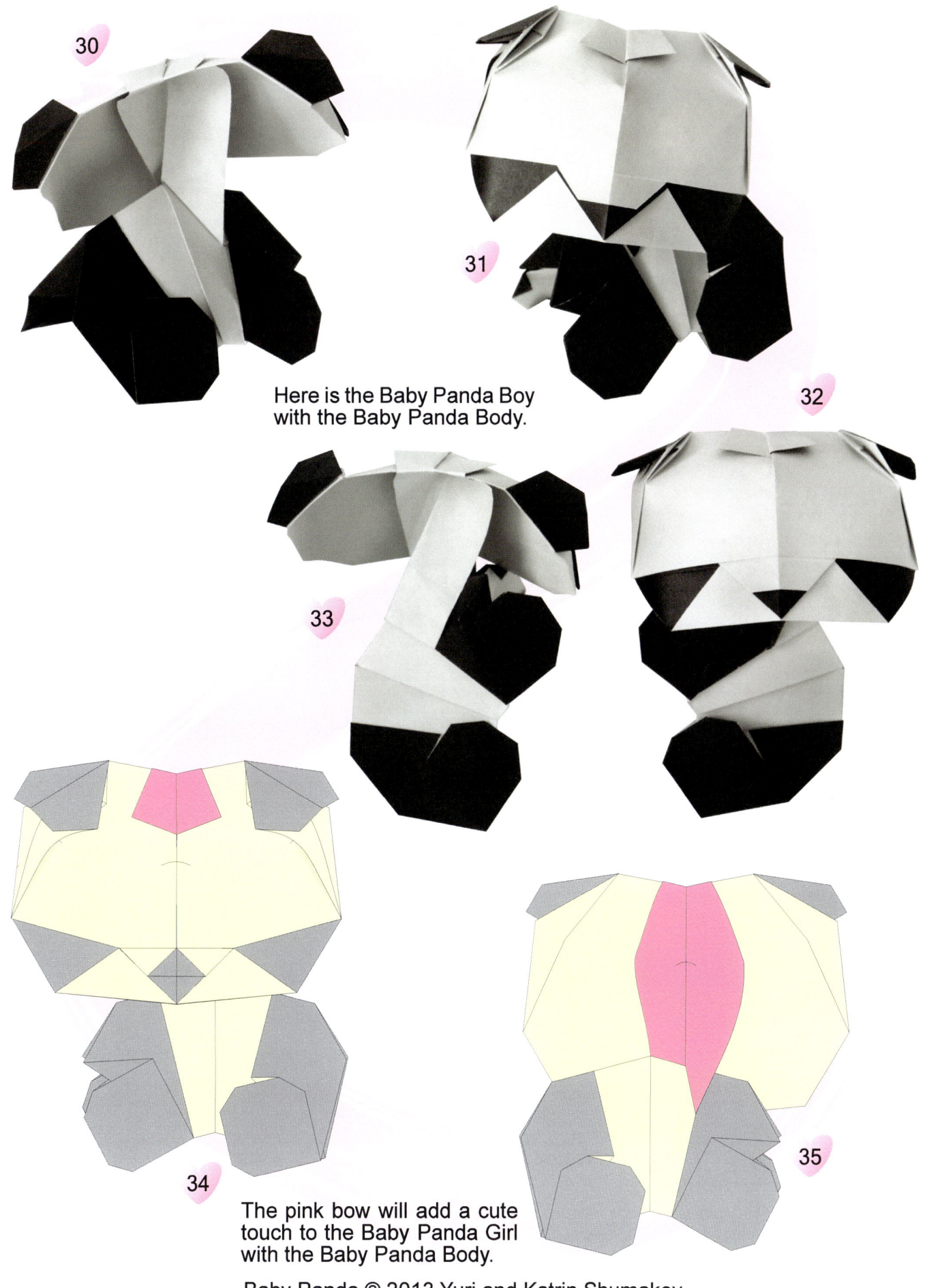

Here is the Baby Panda Boy
with the Baby Panda Body.

The pink bow will add a cute
touch to the Baby Panda Girl
with the Baby Panda Body.

Baby Panda © 2013 Yuri and Katrin Shumakov

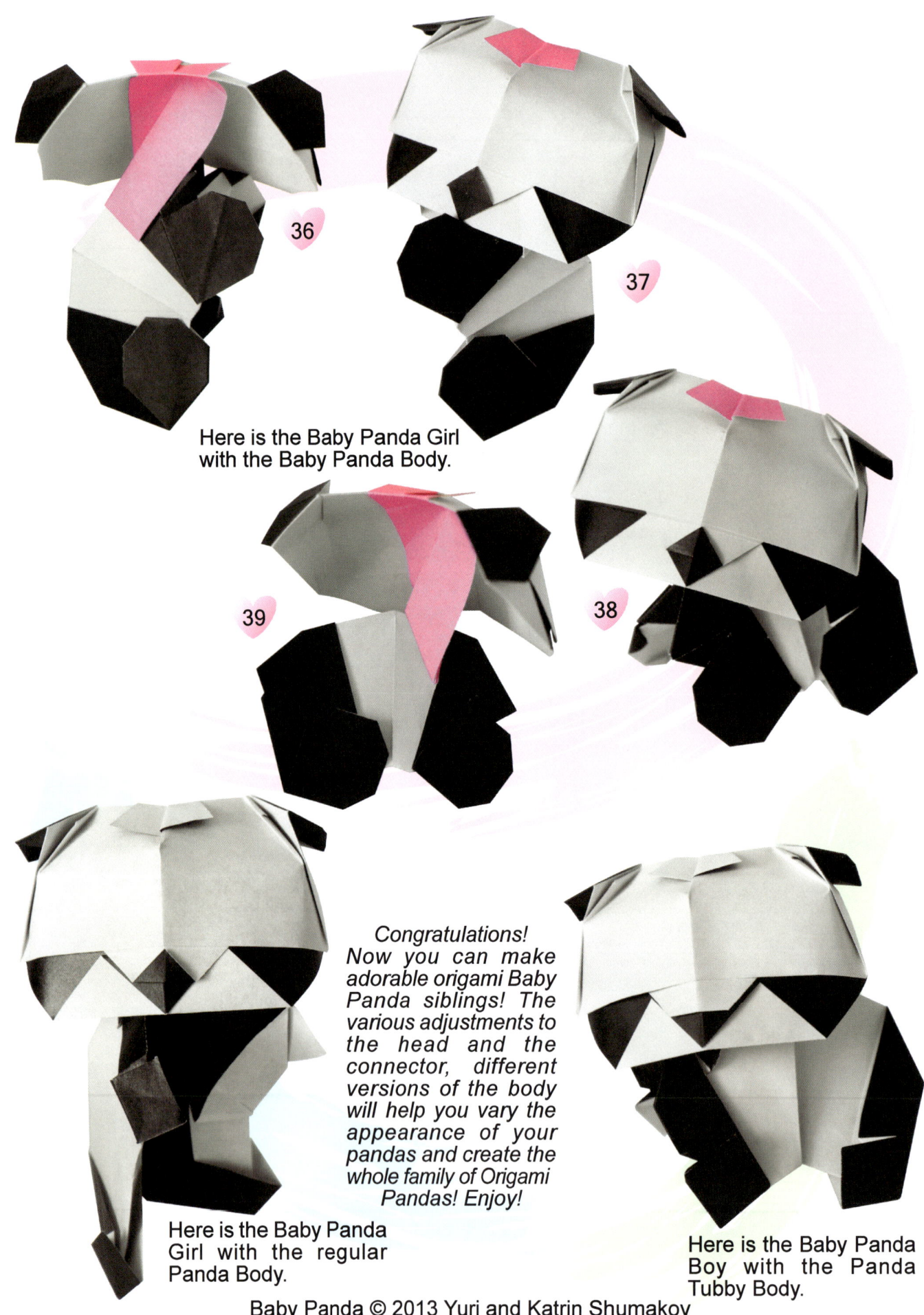

36

37

Here is the Baby Panda Girl with the Baby Panda Body.

39

38

Here is the Baby Panda Girl with the regular Panda Body.

*Congratulations! Now you can make adorable origami Baby Panda siblings! The various adjustments to the head and the connector, different versions of the body will help you vary the appearance of your pandas and create the whole family of Origami Pandas! Enjoy!*

Here is the Baby Panda Boy with the Panda Tubby Body.

Baby Panda © 2013 Yuri and Katrin Shumakov

# Bamboo
## by Katrin Shumakov

The origami bamboo consists of bamboo leaves and tubular stalks that are connected into a plant without any glue. This is a rather simple and flexible design that will allow you to grow a whole origami bamboo forest for your origami panda family.

The flower holder will help to keep the bamboo in a desired position. Follow the diagrams shown on pages 59-62 to fold the holder for your bamboo.

**Suggested paper:** Regular origami paper.

**Suggested sizes:** For each tubular stalk, use a 3-inch (7.5 cm) square. For each leaf, use a half of square used for the stalk, a 1-1/2x3 inches (3.75x7.5cm) rectangle in this case. For a leaf with a long stem, take a strip 1-1/2x6 inches (3.75x15cm).

For the flower holder, you will need a rectangle, 5x10 inches (12.5x25cm) in size, and a strip, 1-1/2x6 inches (3.75x15cm) in size.

To keep the relevant proportion, for the bamboo tubular stalk, it's good to take a quarter of the initial square used for the Mama Panda's Head or Body, which can be a 3-inch (7.5 cm) square - a quarter of a 6-inch (15 cm) square.

If you would like to have the origami panda sitting on one of the sections of the bamboo, then for the bamboo tubular stalk, use a square of the same size as for your Origami Panda's Head or Body.

**Suggested colors:** Shades of green.

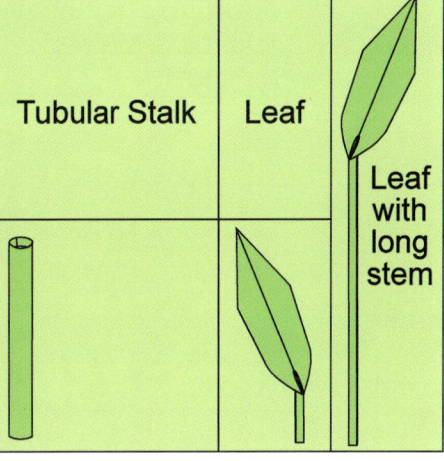

| Tubular Stalk | Leaf | Leaf with long stem |
|---|---|---|

The finished bamboo (with 3 stalk sections) will be about the same height as the longest side of the rectangle used for the flower holder.

Flower Holder

Flower Holder's Ring

Bamboo © 2014 Katrin Shumakov

# Bamboo Leaf

Use a rectangle, 1:2 in proportion.

*Begin with colored side down.*

Valley fold the rectangle in half lengthwise. Press it flat and unfold it.

Valley fold the sides to meet the middle fold-line.

Valley fold the upper side corners to meet the middle fold-line.

Valley fold the sloping edges to meet the middle fold-line. Press them flat and unfold them.

Unfold the flaps.

Open the right-hand flap a bit and inside reverse fold its upper right point along the fold-line made in step 4.

Along the existing fold-line, valley fold the small flap as shown.

This should be the result. Now open the left-hand flap a bit to bring its surface atop, thereby hiding the small flap.

Repeat step 6 for the left-hand side.

Valley fold the small flap as shown.

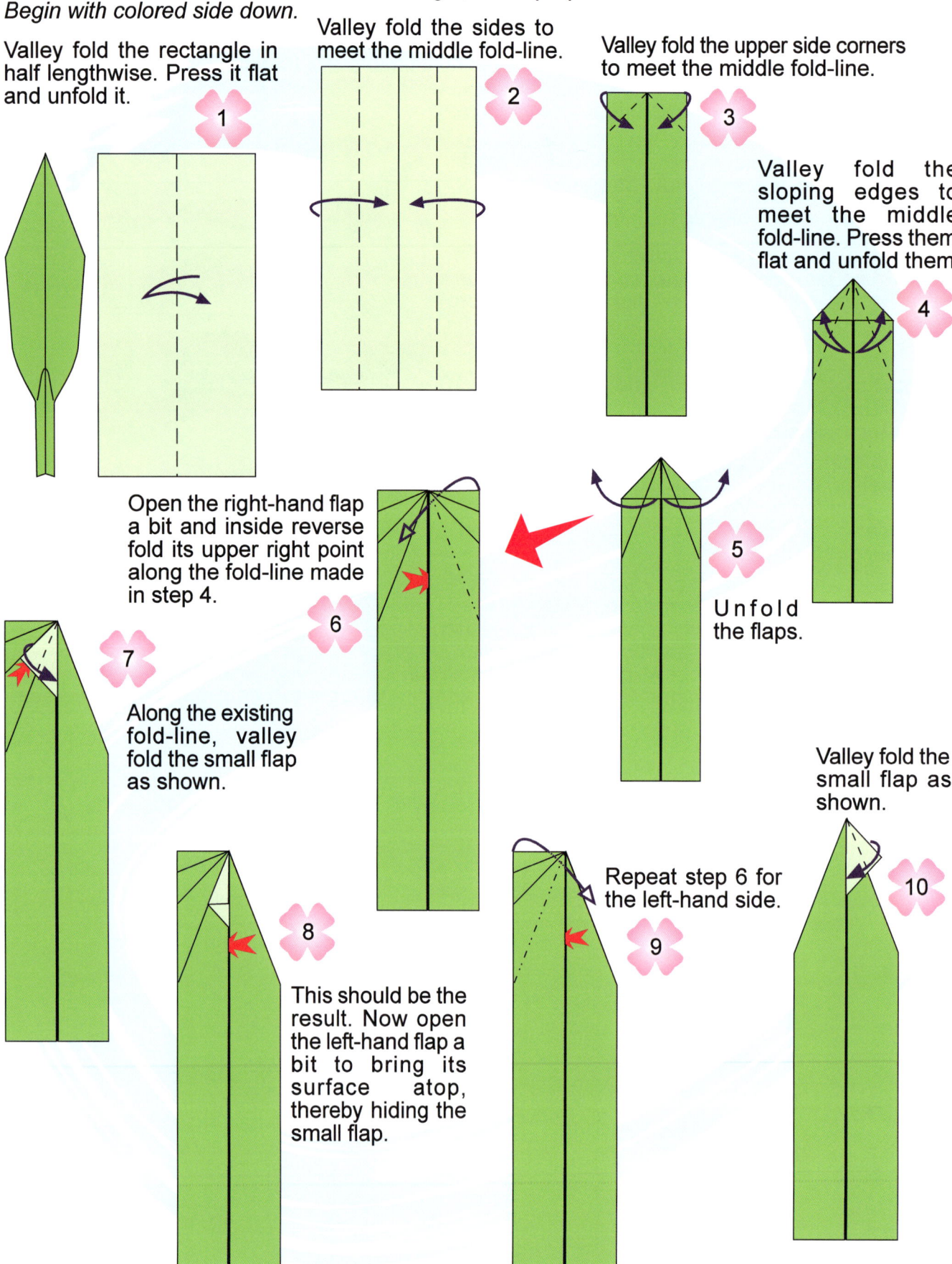

Bamboo © 2014 Katrin Shumakov

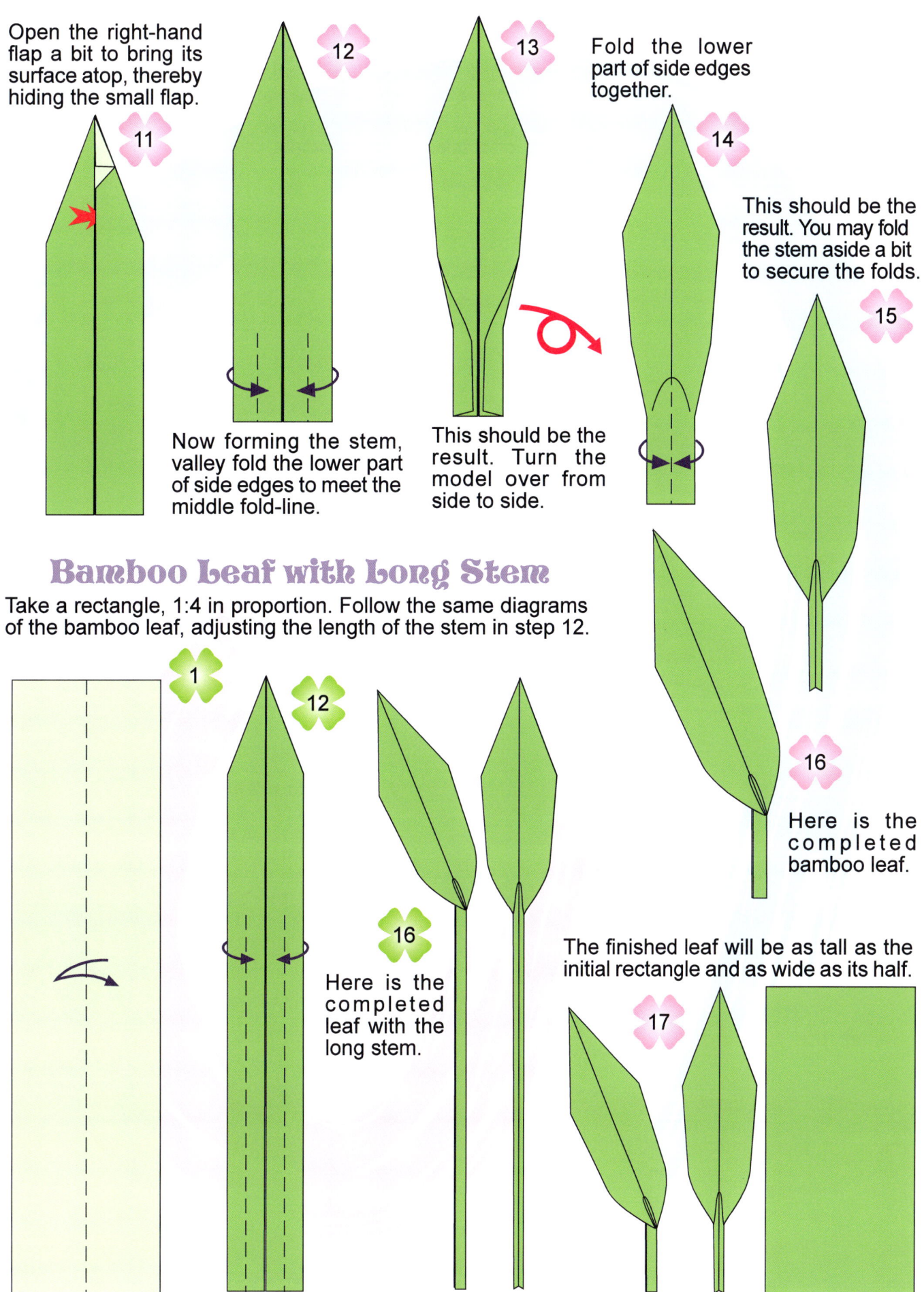

Open the right-hand flap a bit to bring its surface atop, thereby hiding the small flap.

11

12

13

Fold the lower part of side edges together.

14

This should be the result. You may fold the stem aside a bit to secure the folds.

15

Now forming the stem, valley fold the lower part of side edges to meet the middle fold-line.

This should be the result. Turn the model over from side to side.

16

Here is the completed bamboo leaf.

## Bamboo Leaf with Long Stem

Take a rectangle, 1:4 in proportion. Follow the same diagrams of the bamboo leaf, adjusting the length of the stem in step 12.

1

12

16

Here is the completed leaf with the long stem.

The finished leaf will be as tall as the initial rectangle and as wide as its half.

17

Bamboo © 2014 Katrin Shumakov

# Base Tubular Stalk

Use a square of paper. The tubular stalk design uses a rolling technique, so you will also need a thin cylindrical object, for example, a pencil or a plastic knitting-needle. You'll need one such stalk to use in the base of a branch.

*Begin with colored side down.*

**1** Valley fold the top and bottom edges over a little bit, as shown. Press them flat and unfold them.

**2** Start at one side rolling tightly on a thin cylindrical object.

**3** Continue rolling the entire paper, trying to maintain the tightest possible roll.

**4** This should be the result. Unroll the paper.

**5** Start to roll it from the other edge, so that this edge will be inside the tube instead of outside. Now after we rolled it twice, the paper will tend to remain as a tube without glue.

Note the diameter of the base tubular stalk should be wide enough to fit stems of 2-3 leaves and the additional tubular stalk, for reference see step 1 of the bamboo assembly (page 56).

**6** Remove the cylindrical object.

**7** Adjust the tube to a needed diameter. Then, mountain fold the top edge of the stalk, thereby locking it. You may use the same thin cylindrical object to tuck the edge inside. Repeat the locking with the bottom edge of the stalk.

**8** Here is the completed base tubular stalk.

Bamboo © 2014 Katrin Shumakov

# Additional Tubular Stalk

Use a square of paper. You will need as many additional stalks as many sections you would like your bamboo to have above the base stalk.

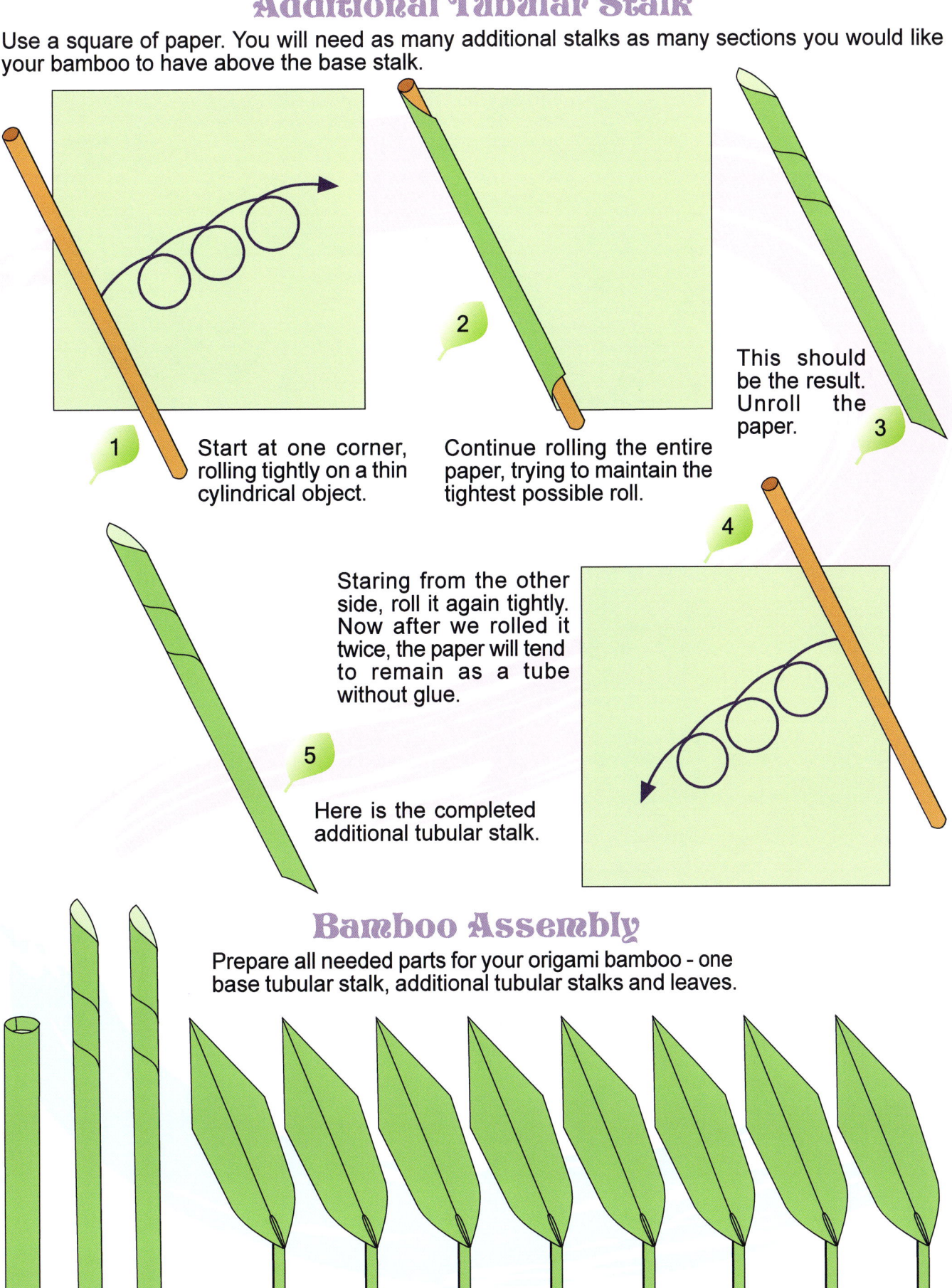

**1** Start at one corner, rolling tightly on a thin cylindrical object.

**2** Continue rolling the entire paper, trying to maintain the tightest possible roll.

**3** This should be the result. Unroll the paper.

**4** Staring from the other side, roll it again tightly. Now after we rolled it twice, the paper will tend to remain as a tube without glue.

**5** Here is the completed additional tubular stalk.

## Bamboo Assembly

Prepare all needed parts for your origami bamboo - one base tubular stalk, additional tubular stalks and leaves.

Bamboo © 2014 Katrin Shumakov

Note the lower part of the additional tubular stalk can be rolled tighter while its top can be wider to fit the next level's stalks.

**2**

**1**

Starting from the base of the plant, insert stems of 2 or 3 leaves into the base tubular stalk. Then secure their position by inserting the additional tubular stalk.

**3**

This should be the result. Now mountain fold the raw edge of the additional stalk. You may use the thin cylindrical object you used for rolling to tuck the edge inside.

Now insert the next level of leaves into the tubular stalk and the additional tubular stalk. Then, repeat step 3 to lock the raw edge of the stalk.

**4**

Bamboo © 2014 Katrin Shumakov

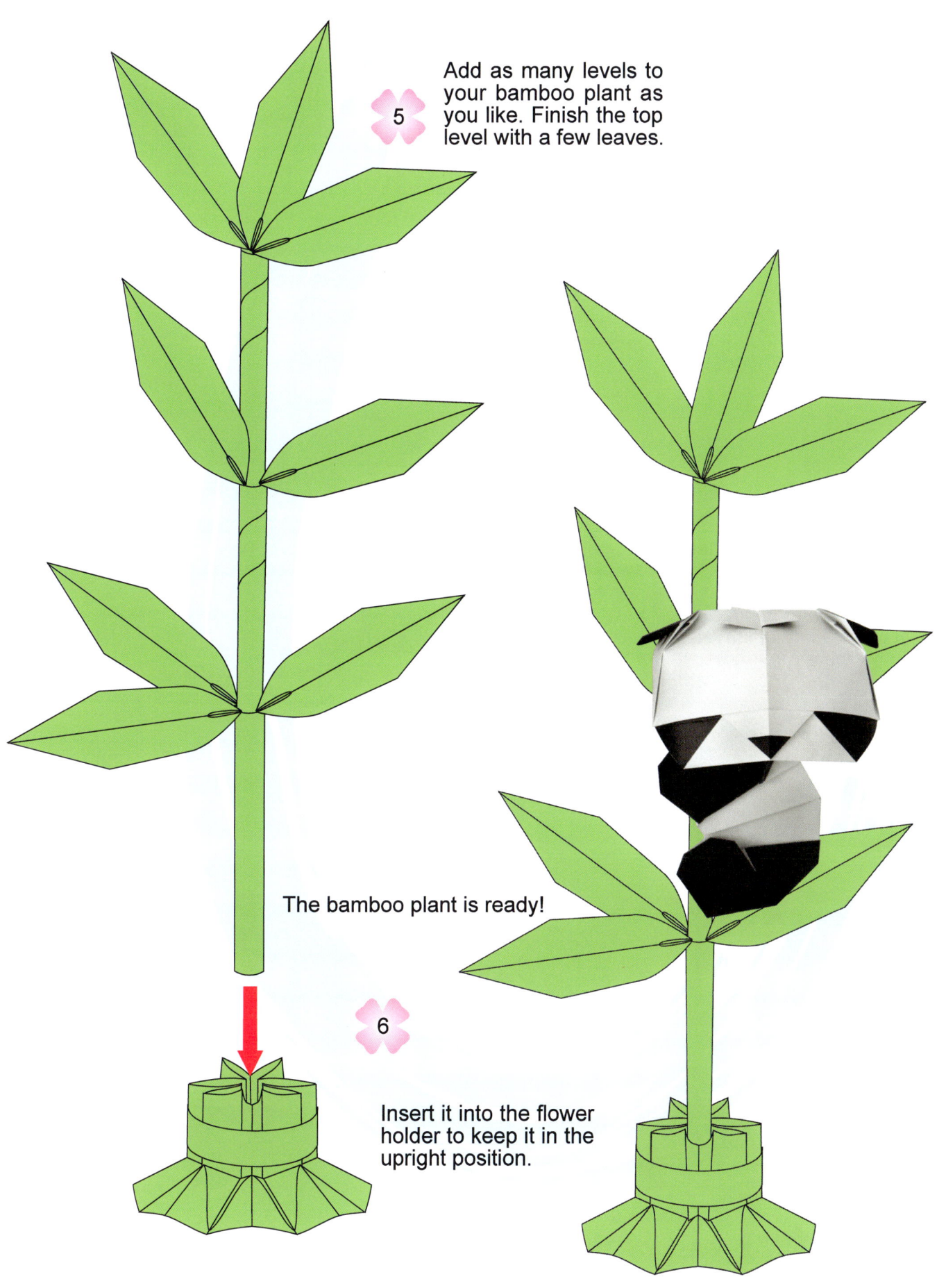

**5** Add as many levels to your bamboo plant as you like. Finish the top level with a few leaves.

The bamboo plant is ready!

**6**

Insert it into the flower holder to keep it in the upright position.

Bamboo © 2014 Katrin Shumakov

**7** You may add the leaves with long stems as new sprouts.

Here is the completed bamboo plant.

**8**

*Congratulations!*
*Now you can grow a whole origami bamboo forest for your origami panda family! Vary the quantity of leaves and levels to create different configurations of the origami bamboo. Enjoy!*

Add new sprouts right into the holder or on the top level.

Bamboo © 2014 Katrin Shumakov

# Flower Holder
## by Katrin Shumakov

This design is very useful for keeping the plant stalks and branches in a vertical position and in a fixed order. The flower holder will help to arrange you origami bamboo in a desired position.

**Suggested paper:** Regular origami paper.

**Suggested sizes:** Use a rectangle, 1:2 in proportion, for instance, 5x10 inches (12.5x25cm) in size. Also you will need a strip, 1-1/2x6 inches (3.75x15cm) in size for the flower holder's ring.

**Suggested colors:** All shades of green.

Flower Holder

Flower Holder's Ring

The diameter of the finished holder will be about a half of the short side of the original rectangle.

*Begin with the colored side up.*

Divide the rectangle into 8 equal vertical sections by valley folding. Press the folds flat and unfold them. Then, turn the paper over.

**1**

This time, divide each vertical section in half by valley folding.

**2**

Working from the bottom left-hand corner, make the diagonal fold-mark in the first section. Then, valley fold the bottom edge up, so that the fold-line passes over the top of the diagonal fold-mark, as shown.

**3**

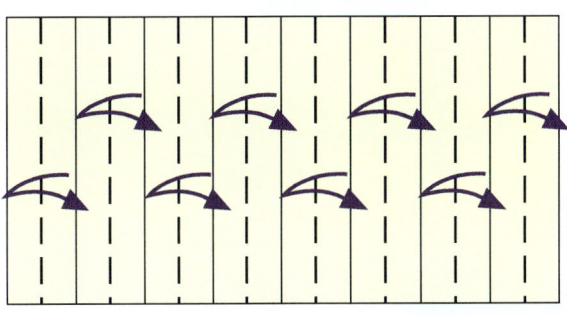

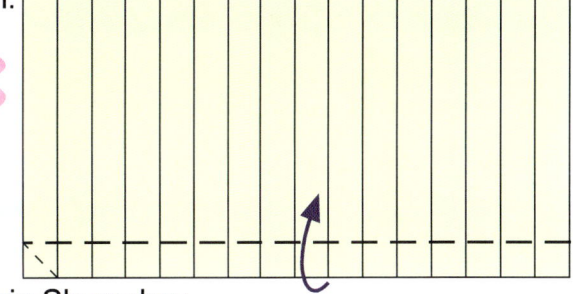

Flower Holder © 1996 Katrin Shumakov

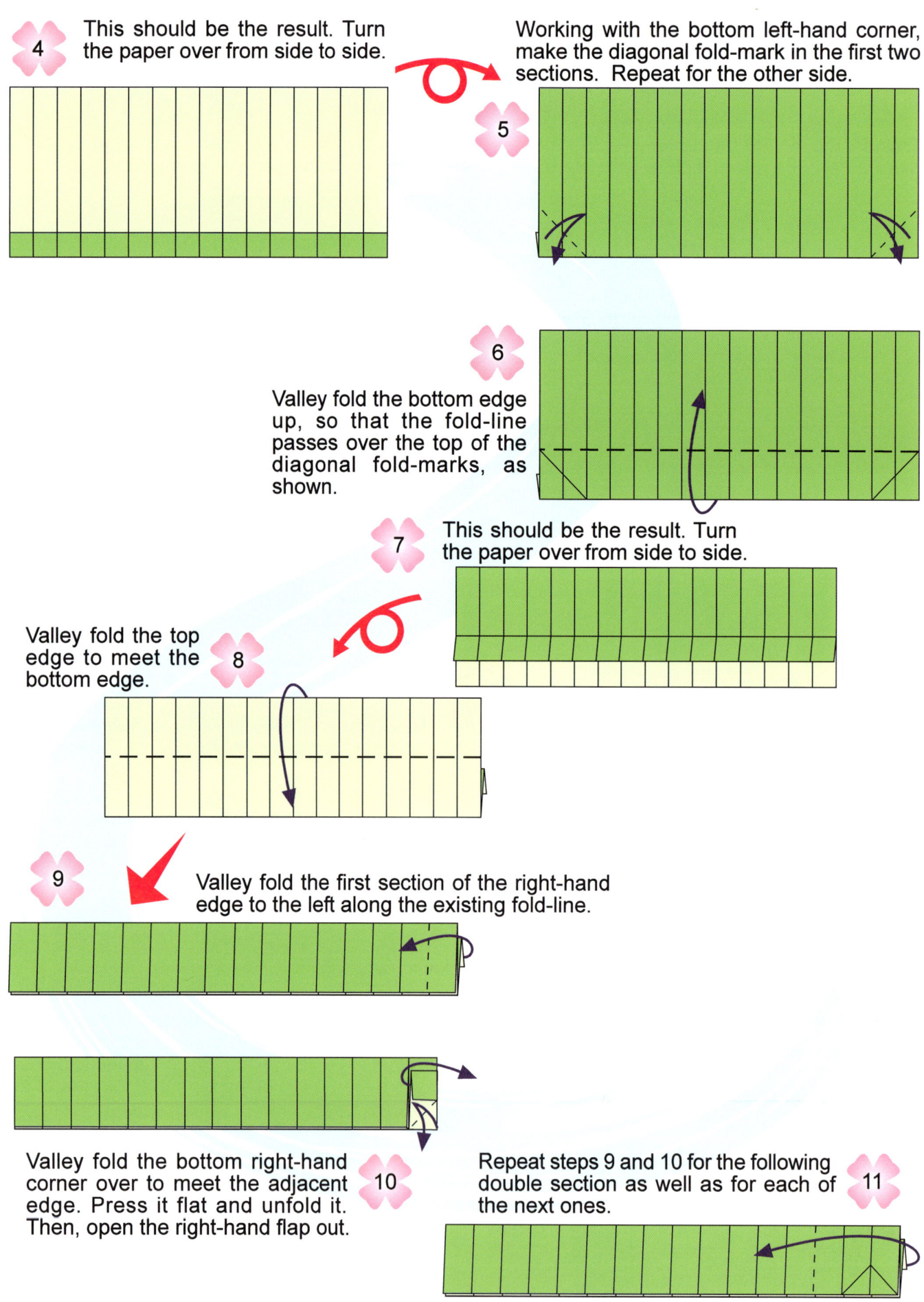

**4** This should be the result. Turn the paper over from side to side.

**5** Working with the bottom left-hand corner, make the diagonal fold-mark in the first two sections. Repeat for the other side.

**6** Valley fold the bottom edge up, so that the fold-line passes over the top of the diagonal fold-marks, as shown.

**7** This should be the result. Turn the paper over from side to side.

**8** Valley fold the top edge to meet the bottom edge.

**9** Valley fold the first section of the right-hand edge to the left along the existing fold-line.

**10** Valley fold the bottom right-hand corner over to meet the adjacent edge. Press it flat and unfold it. Then, open the right-hand flap out.

**11** Repeat steps 9 and 10 for the following double section as well as for each of the next ones.

Flower Holder © 1996 Katrin Shumakov

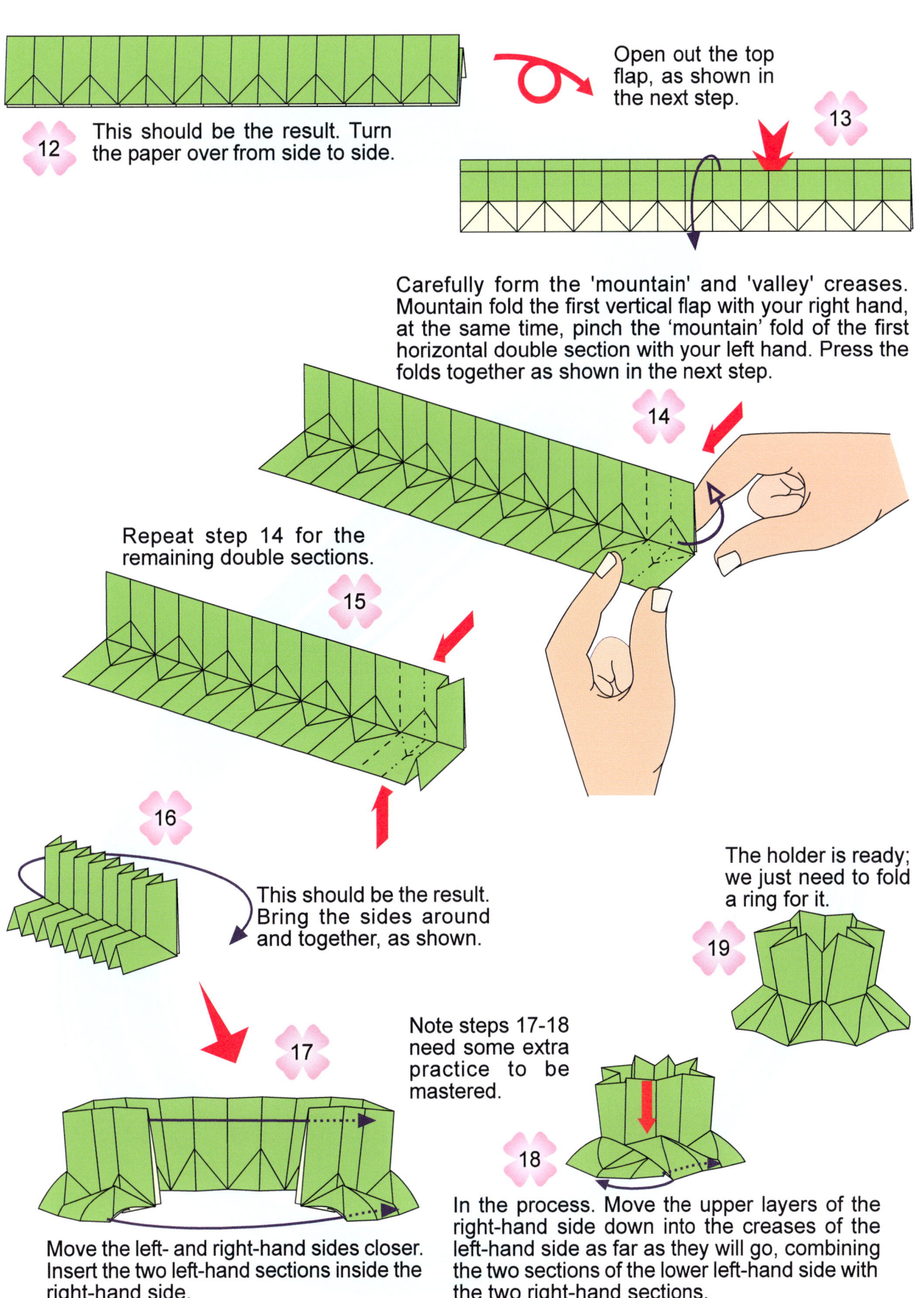

**12** This should be the result. Turn the paper over from side to side.

Open out the top flap, as shown in the next step.

**13**

Carefully form the 'mountain' and 'valley' creases. Mountain fold the first vertical flap with your right hand, at the same time, pinch the 'mountain' fold of the first horizontal double section with your left hand. Press the folds together as shown in the next step.

**14**

Repeat step 14 for the remaining double sections.

**15**

**16** This should be the result. Bring the sides around and together, as shown.

The holder is ready; we just need to fold a ring for it.

**19**

Note steps 17-18 need some extra practice to be mastered.

**17**

**18**

Move the left- and right-hand sides closer. Insert the two left-hand sections inside the right-hand side.

In the process. Move the upper layers of the right-hand side down into the creases of the left-hand side as far as they will go, combining the two sections of the lower left-hand side with the two right-hand sections.

Flower Holder © 1996 Katrin Shumakov

# Ring & Assembly

**1** Take a strip of paper, long enough to fit around the compressed middle section of the holder, plus a little more.

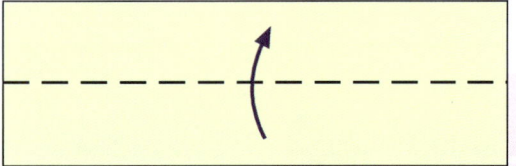

Valley fold the paper in half from bottom to top. Press the paper flat.

**2** Valley fold the paper in half from bottom to top. Press it flat and unfold it.

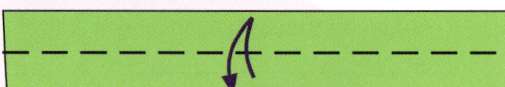

**3**

Bring the side ends together and insert one end inside the other, thereby shaping the strip into a circle of the necessary size.

Adjust the diameter of the ring if needed. Remove the ring.

**4** Now try the ring on the compressed middle section of the holder.

**5**

**6** Mountain fold the top edge of the ring, thereby locking the ring.

**7** Here is the completed ring.

Compress the middle of the holder and slip the ring on to the compressed middle section, thereby locking it.

**8**

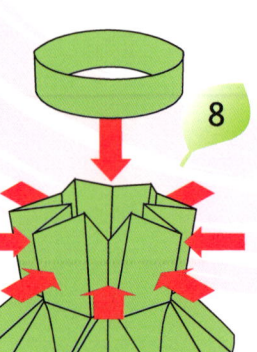

**10** Here is the completed flower holder.

**9** This should be the result. Open out the layers of each section of the flower holder slightly, thereby releasing some space for plant stems.

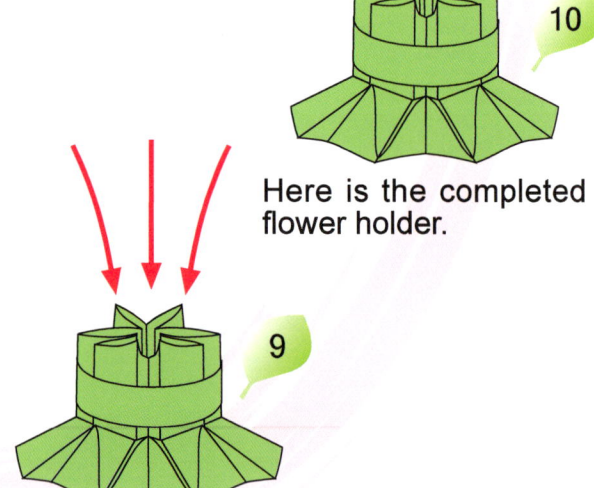

Flower Holder © 1996 Katrin Shumakov

# Cherry Blossom Tree
## by Katrin Shumakov

The cute cherry blossom tree consists of flowers, flat stalks and tubular stalks that are connected into a plant without any glue. This is a fun and flexible design that will allow you to grow a blossoming origami cherry orchard for your origami panda family.

The flower holder will help to keep the tree in a desired position. Follow the diagrams shown on pages 59-62 to fold the flower holder for your cherry blossom tree.

**Suggested sizes:** Use a 3-inch (7.5 cm) or a 2-1/2 inch (5cm) square for each flower.

For each tubular stalk, use a 3-inch (7.5 cm) square. For each flat stalk, use a strip, which is about 1/4 of the square used for the tubular stalk, a 7/8x3 inches (2x7.5cm) rectangle in this case.

For the flower holder, you will need a rectangle, 5x10 inches (12.5x25cm) in size, and a strip, 1-1/2x6 inches (3.75x15cm) in size.

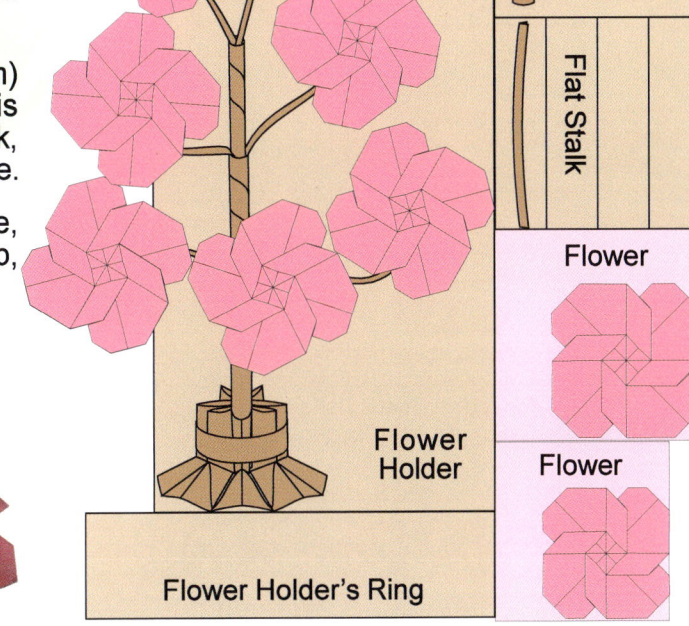

**Suggested paper:** Regular origami paper.

**Suggested colors:** Pink for blossoms, brown or green for stalks and the holder.

The diameter of the finished flower will be about 3/4 of the side of the initial square. The finished tree (with 3 stalk sections) will be about the same height as the longest side of the rectangle used for the flower holder.

Give the flower to the sitting Origami Panda. Insert the flower's stalk into Panda's hand, between the layers, like into the pocket, and balance it there.

Cherry Blossom Tree © 1998 Katrin Shumakov

# Flower

This simple design of a flower with 4 petals can play a role of a symbolic cherry blossom.

Use a square of paper.

*Begin with colored side up.*

Valley fold the square in half from corner to corner and make the diagonal fold-line. Unfold it. Make the second diagonal fold-line. Then, turn the paper over.

Valley fold the square in half from side to side. Press the fold flat and unfold it. Repeat in another direction.

Bring the sides together and down towards you. Press the paper down neatly, thereby making a shape that, in origami, is called the preliminary fold.

Press the fold flat and unfold the flap.

Working with all the layers, valley fold the right-hand upper sloping edge over, so that the top point touches the middle point of the left-hand upper edge, as shown.

This should be the result. Now turn the model over from side to side.

Repeat steps 4 and 5 for this side also, thereby folding the right-hand upper sloping edge over the intersection of lines, as shown. Press it flat and unfold the flap.

Valley fold the top point down to meet the intersection of folds. Press the fold flat and unfold it.

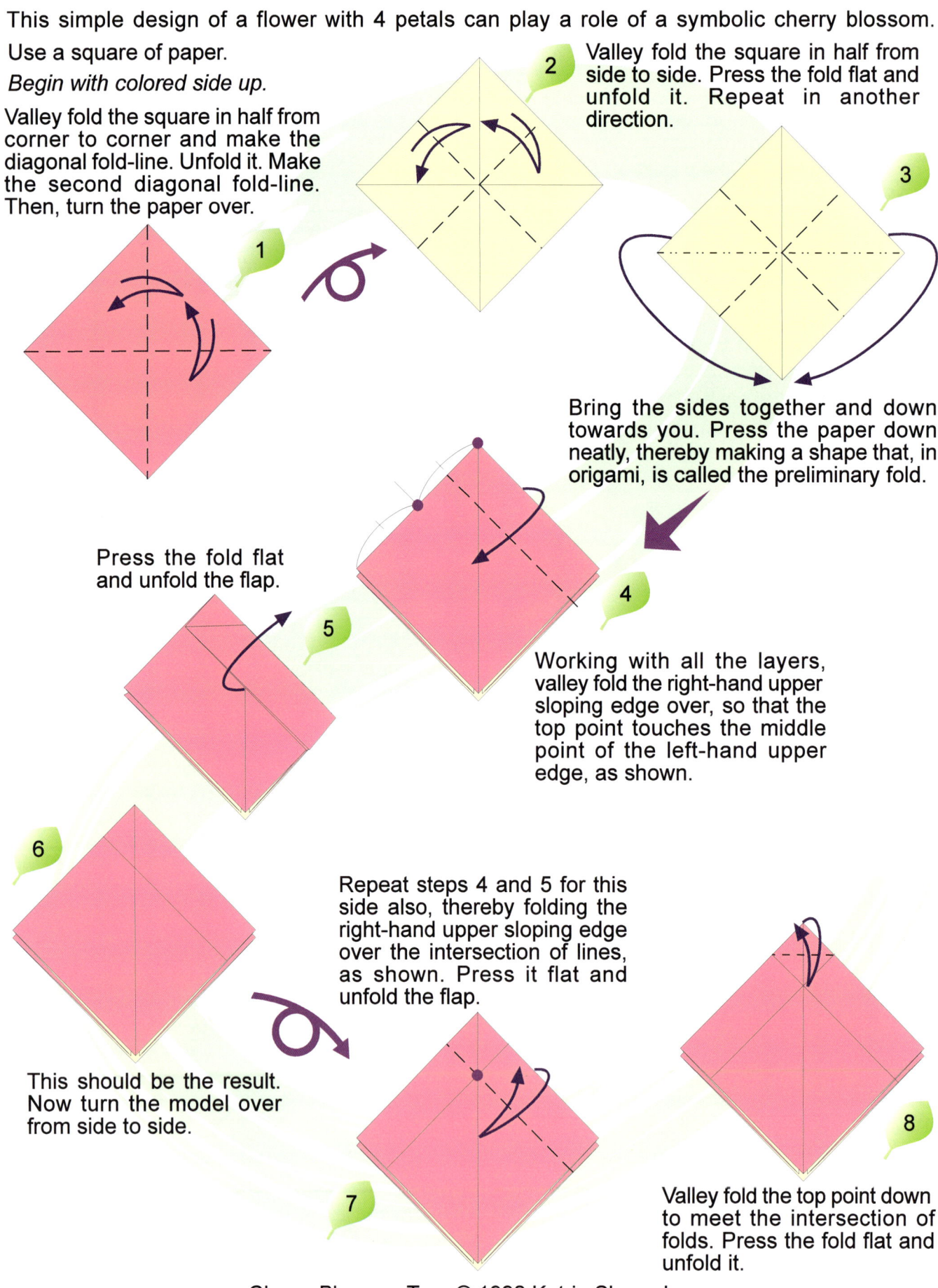

Cherry Blossom Tree © 1998 Katrin Shumakov

Open the model from the bottom and flatten the top point, creasing four sides of the inner square into mountain folds, so it looks like a table top as shown in the next step.

9

10

Now pinch the sides as shown and twist them clockwise around the top square, at the same time opening the model from the bottom and bringing it into the position shown in the next step.

This should be the result.

11

Valley fold and unfold the corners of the resulted flaps as shown.

12

Inside reverse fold each pre-folded corner along the fold-line made in the previous step.

13

14

This should be the result. Now turn the paper over.

15

Working with the side corner on each quarter, valley fold it over as shown.

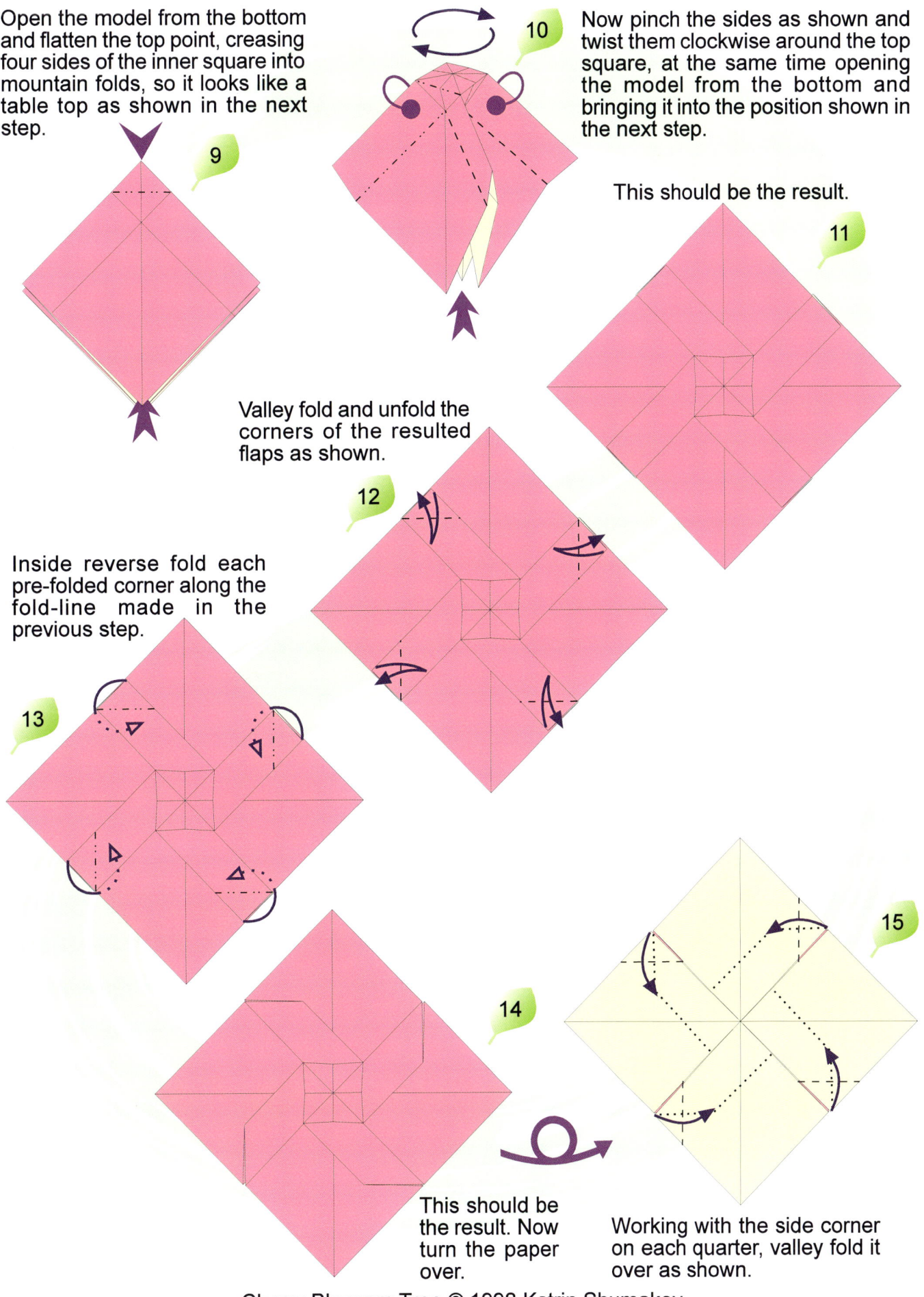

Cherry Blossom Tree © 1998 Katrin Shumakov

**16** This should be the result. Turn the model over.

**17** Mountain fold the tips as shown, thereby making the petals more round.

**18** The flower is ready!

The diagrams of folding the flat stalk are shown on the next page.

To add a stalk to the flower, insert the tip of the flat stalk under the layer. You can open the layers a bit and direct the stalk's tip right into the middle.

**19**

**20** Here is the completed 4-petal flower on a stalk.

This cute design of a 4-petal flower also resembles a simple rose. You may use it separately to make a little flower garden for your Origami Panda Family.

Cherry Blossom Tree © 1998 Katrin Shumakov

You can vary the proportions of the flower center and petals, adjusting the position of the fold-line in step 4 (page 64). For instance, you may fold the right-hand upper sloping edge over, so that the top point touches the 2/3 of the left-hand upper edge, as shown. It will result in a bigger center of the flower.

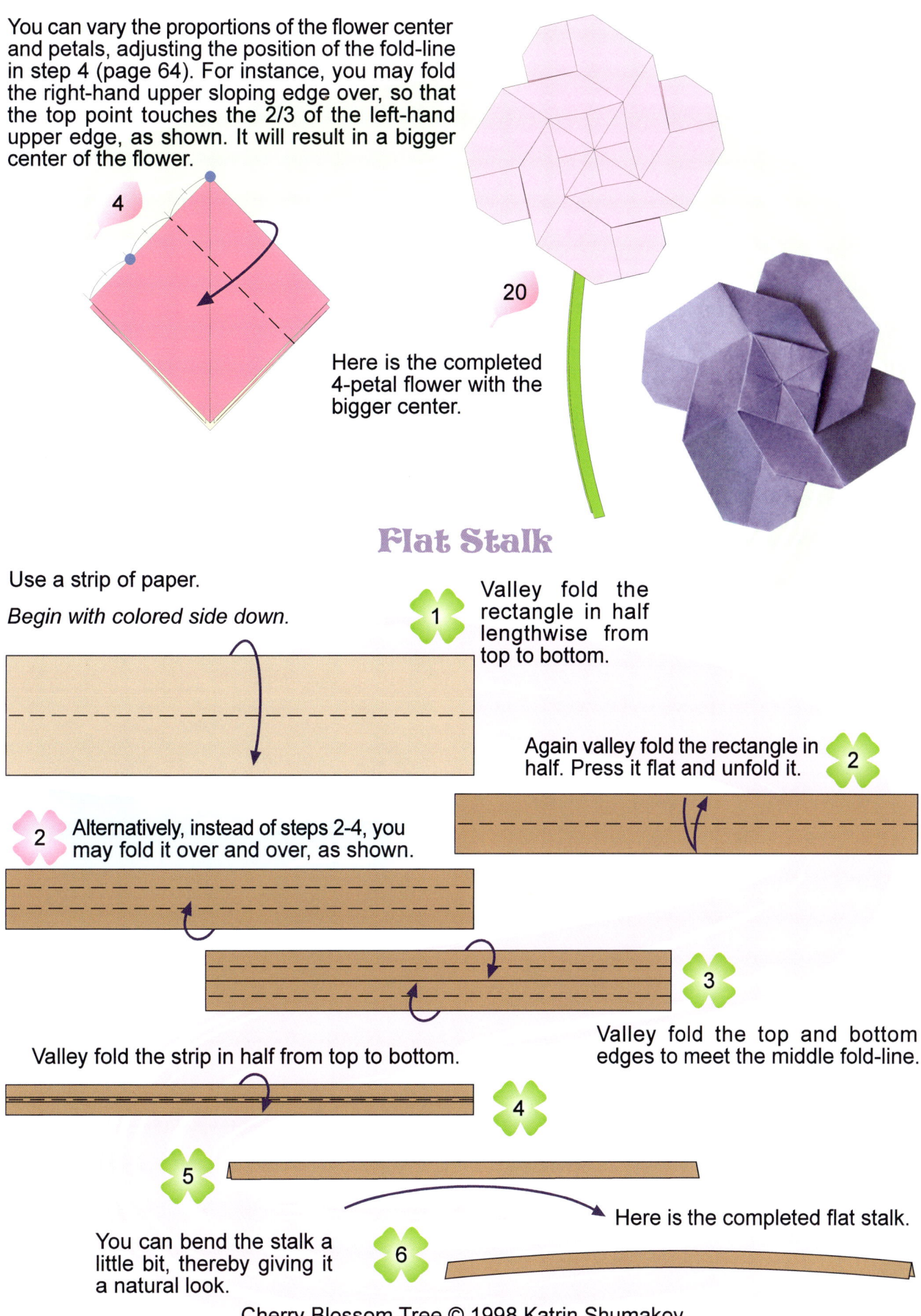

**4**

**20**

Here is the completed 4-petal flower with the bigger center.

## Flat Stalk

Use a strip of paper.

*Begin with colored side down.*

**1** Valley fold the rectangle in half lengthwise from top to bottom.

**2** Again valley fold the rectangle in half. Press it flat and unfold it.

**2** Alternatively, instead of steps 2-4, you may fold it over and over, as shown.

**3** Valley fold the top and bottom edges to meet the middle fold-line.

Valley fold the strip in half from top to bottom.

**4**

**5**

Here is the completed flat stalk.

**6** You can bend the stalk a little bit, thereby giving it a natural look.

Cherry Blossom Tree © 1998 Katrin Shumakov

# Cherry Blossom Tree Assembly

Prepare all needed parts for your origami cherry blossom tree - one base tubular stalk, additional tubular stalks, flat stalks and flowers.

Follow the diagrams shown on pages 54-55 to fold the base tubular stalk and additional tubular stalks for your cherry blossom tree.

**1**
Starting from the base of the tree, insert 2 or 3 flat stalks into the base tubular stalk and secure their position by inserting the additional tubular stalk.

**2**
Note the lower part of the additional tubular stalk can be rolled tighter while its top can be wider to fit the next level's stalks.

Cherry Blossom Tree © 1998 Katrin Shumakov

This should be the result. Bend the flat stalks a little to give them a natural look.

**3**

**4**

Now mountain fold the raw edge of the additional stalk. You may use the thin cylindrical object you used for rolling to tuck the edge inside.

**5**

Forming the next level, insert flat stalks into the tubular stalk. Then add the additional tubular stalk.

**6**

Lock the raw edge of the additional stalk. You may use the thin cylindrical object, you used for rolling, to tuck the edge inside.

Cherry Blossom Tree © 1998 Katrin Shumakov

**7** Add as many levels to your tree as you like, finishing the top level with a few flat stalks.

This should be the result. The structure of your cherry blossom tree is completed; we just need to set it up and add some blooms.

**9** Insert the trunk into the flower holder to keep it in the upright position.

**8**

Cherry Blossom Tree © 1998 Katrin Shumakov

**10**

Now let's make your tree blossom! Add a flower to each flat stalk, inserting its tip under the layer in the middle of the back side of the flower.

**11**

Here is the completed Cherry Blossom Tree.

*Congratulations! Now you can grow a whole origami cherry orchard for your origami pandas! Vary the quantity of flowers and levels, play with color combinations to create different appearances of the origami cherry blossom trees. Enjoy!*

Cherry Blossom Tree © 1998 Katrin Shumakov

# Simple Tulip
## by Katrin Shumakov

This simple and cute design of a tulip is fun to fold and is perfect to give your Origami Mama Panda on Mother's Day. The tulip folds from a square of paper. You also will need a strip of paper to make a stalk for it or a leaf with a stalk.

**Suggested paper:** Regular origami paper.

**Suggested sizes:** Use a 3-inch (7.5 cm) square for a tulip. For a stalk, take a strip of a desired length, say, 1/4 of the initial square used for a flower or so. For a leaf with a stem, use a strip, 1-1/2x6 inches (3.75x15cm) in size.

**Suggested colors:** Red, pink, yellow or any color you like.

When folding the tulip for your Origami Mama Panda, you may use a quarter of the initial square used for the Panda's Head to receive the flower in proportions pictured here.

The finished flower will be a quarter of the side of the initial square.

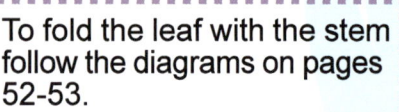

To fold the leaf with the stem follow the diagrams on pages 52-53.

The diagrams of folding the flat stalk are shown on page 67.

Present the tulip to the sitting Origami Panda! Insert the flower's stalk into Panda's hand, between the layers, like into the pocket, and balance it there.

Simple Tulip © 2014 Katrin Shumakov

# Flower

Use a square of paper.

*Begin with colored side up.*

Valley fold the square in half from side to side. Press the fold flat and unfold it. Repeat in another direction. Then, turn the paper over.

**1**

**2** Valley fold the square in half from corner to corner and make the diagonal fold-line. Unfold it. Make the second diagonal fold-line.

**3** Bring the sides together and down towards you. Press the top down neatly into a triangle, thereby completing the shape that in origami is called the balloon base.

**4** This should be the result. Insert the stalk under the front layer as far as it will go.

**5** Working with the front flaps, valley fold the side corners up about 1/3 of the way as shown and so that the folds secure the stalk.

**6** Now mountain fold the left- and right-hand points back, thereby shaping the tulip on the front side.

**7** This should be the result. Now turn the model over from side to side.

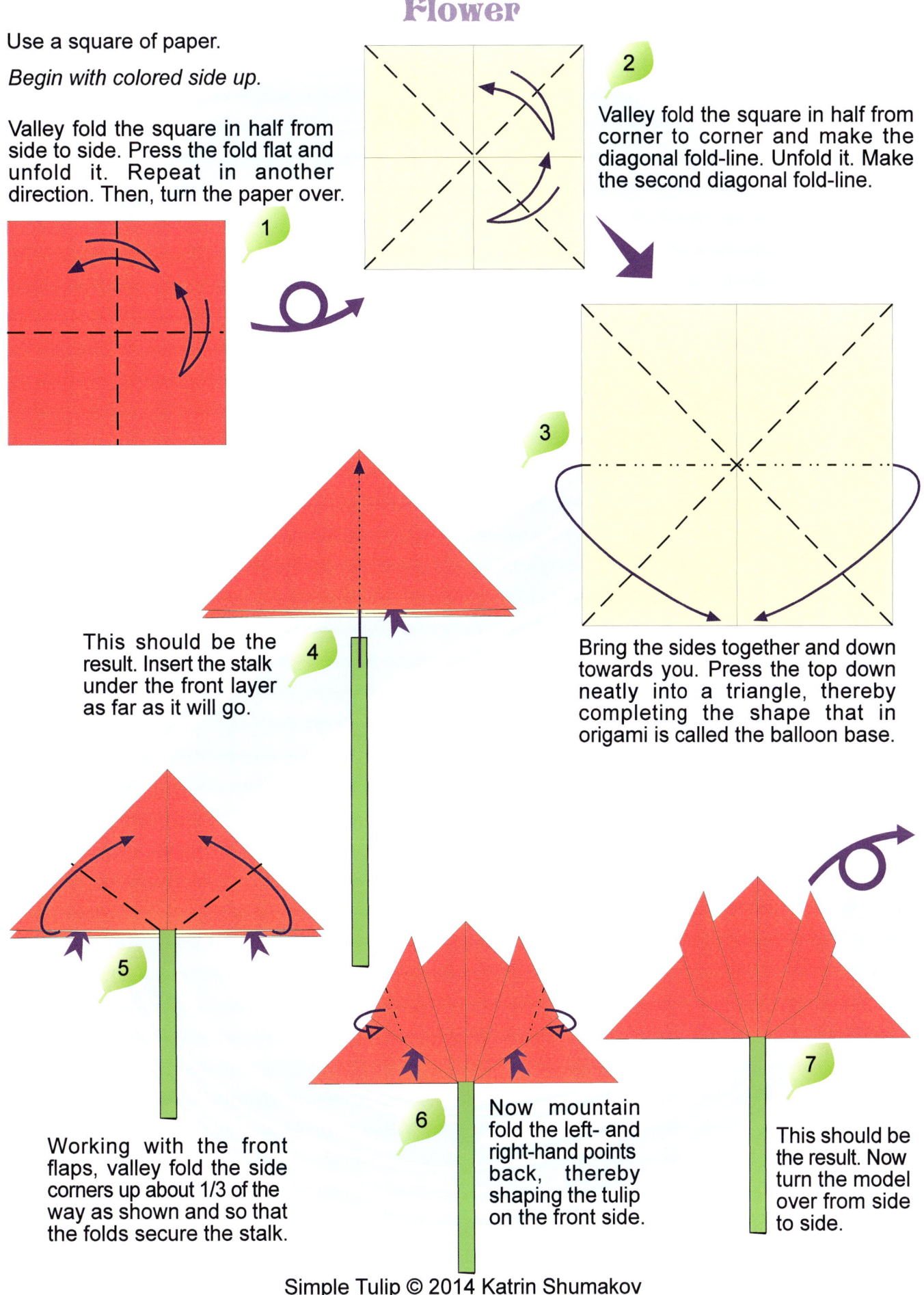

Simple Tulip © 2014 Katrin Shumakov

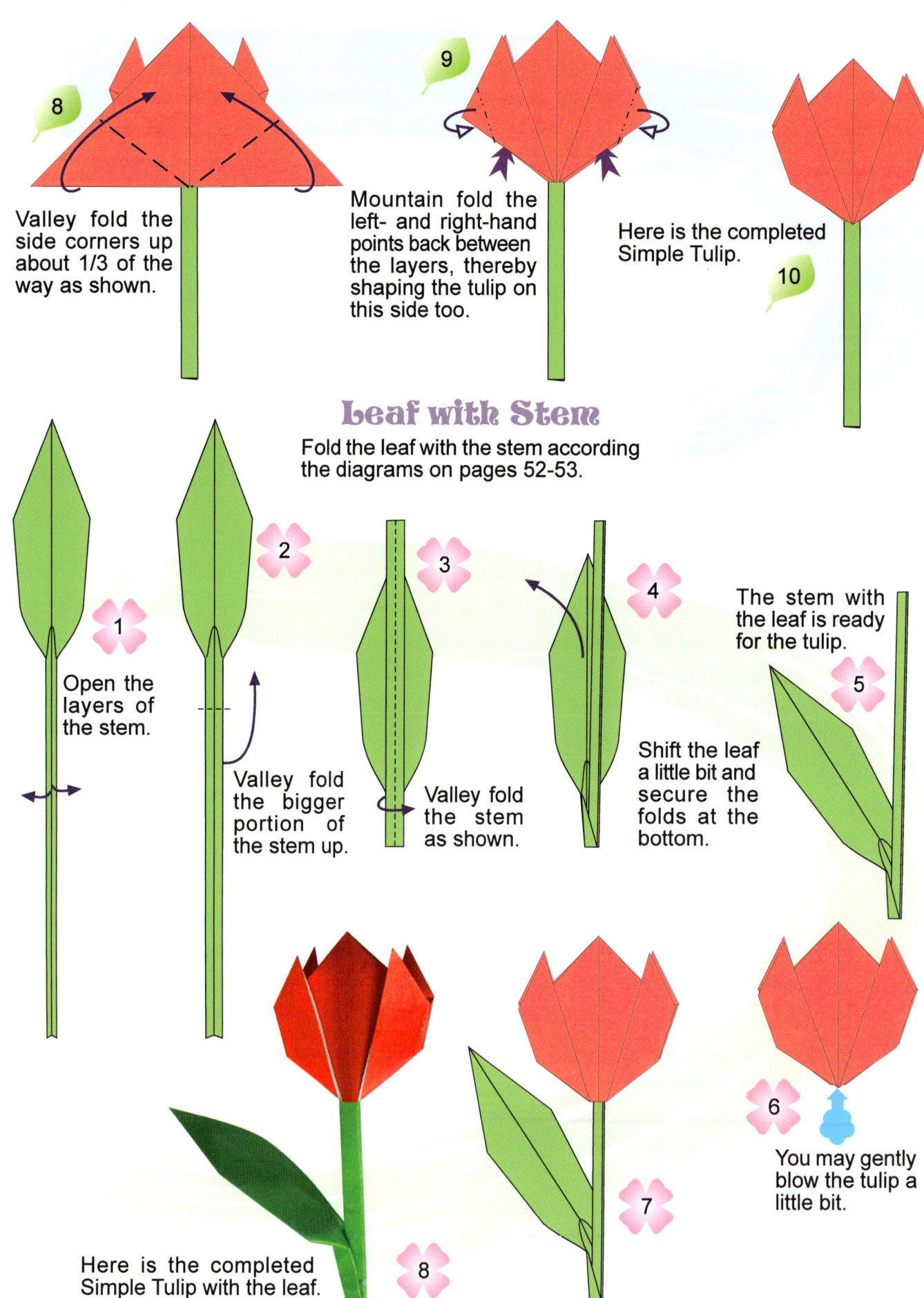

**8** Valley fold the side corners up about 1/3 of the way as shown.

**9** Mountain fold the left- and right-hand points back between the layers, thereby shaping the tulip on this side too.

**10** Here is the completed Simple Tulip.

## Leaf with Stem

Fold the leaf with the stem according the diagrams on pages 52-53.

**1** Open the layers of the stem.

**2** Valley fold the bigger portion of the stem up.

**3** Valley fold the stem as shown.

**4** Shift the leaf a little bit and secure the folds at the bottom.

**5** The stem with the leaf is ready for the tulip.

**6** You may gently blow the tulip a little bit.

**7**

**8** Here is the completed Simple Tulip with the leaf.

Simple Tulip © 2014 Katrin Shumakov

# Heart Balloon
## by Yuri Shumakov

This is a fun design to complement origami pandas and make origami scenes of their life. The heart balloon folds from a square of paper. You also will need a strip, 1:4 in proportion, to make a thread / thin stick to keep the balloon on.

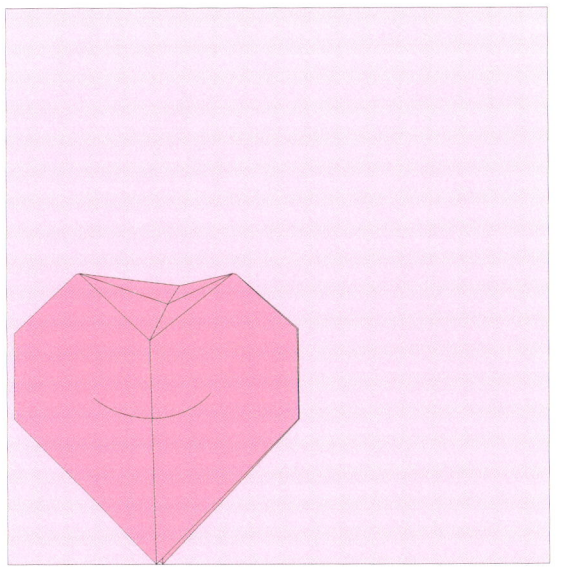

**Suggested paper:** Regular origami paper.

**Suggested sizes:** Use a 6-inch (15 cm) square and a strip 1-1/2x6 inches (3.75x15cm). Or a 5-inch (12.5 cm) square and a strip 1-1/4x5 inches (3x12.5cm).

To be in the relevant proportion to the panda design, the heart balloon has to be folded from a square of the same size as used to fold the panda head or body.

**Suggested colors:** Red, pink or blue will do nicely.

The finished heart will be about a quarter of the initial square as pictured.

Give the heart balloons to the sitting Origami Pandas to play with. The thread/stick of the heart balloon can be inserted into Panda's hand, between the layers, like into the pocket, and balanced there.

Heart Balloon © 2014 Yuri Shumakov

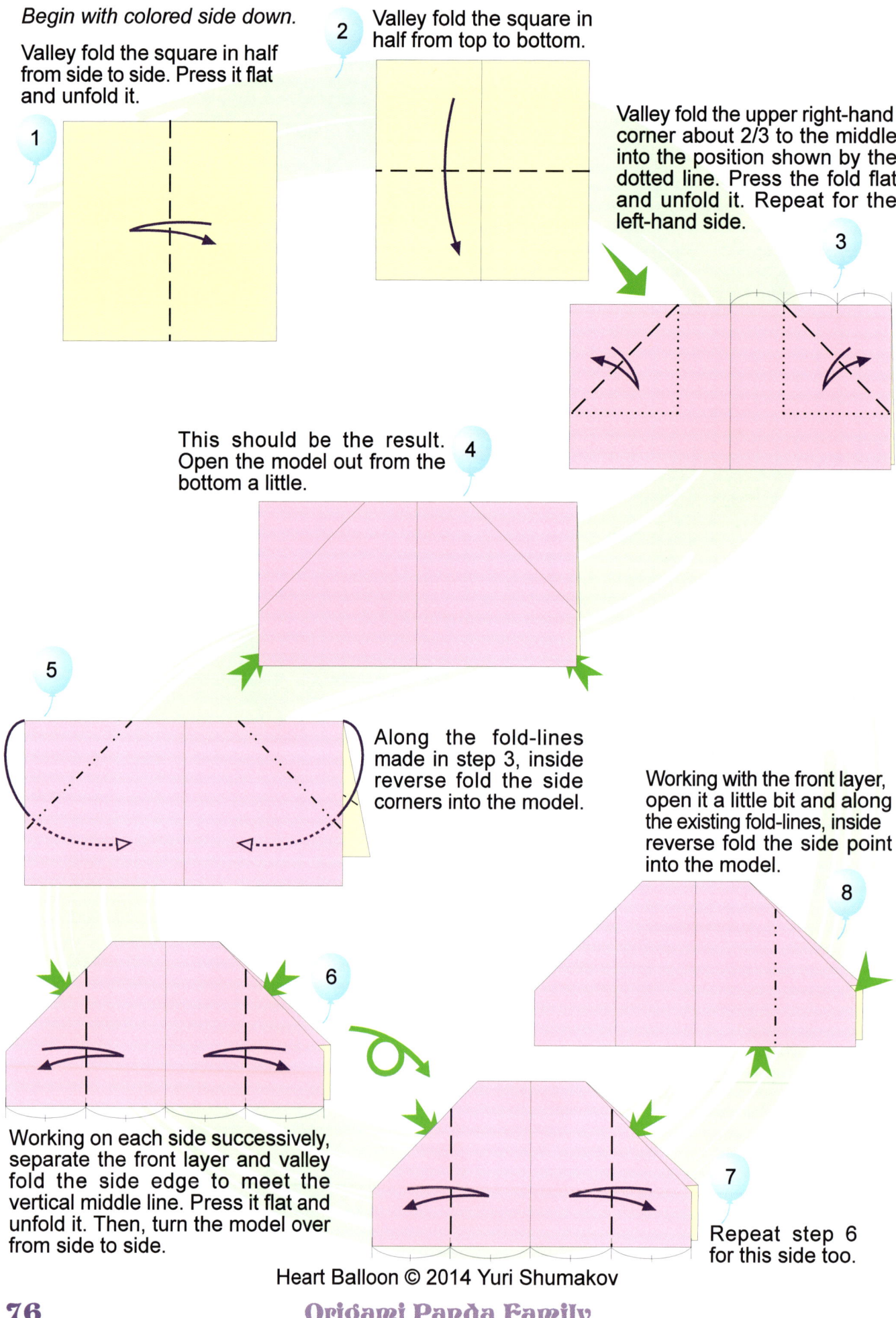

**Begin with colored side down.**

**1** Valley fold the square in half from side to side. Press it flat and unfold it.

**2** Valley fold the square in half from top to bottom.

**3** Valley fold the upper right-hand corner about 2/3 to the middle into the position shown by the dotted line. Press the fold flat and unfold it. Repeat for the left-hand side.

**4** This should be the result. Open the model out from the bottom a little.

**5** Along the fold-lines made in step 3, inside reverse fold the side corners into the model.

**6** Working on each side successively, separate the front layer and valley fold the side edge to meet the vertical middle line. Press it flat and unfold it. Then, turn the model over from side to side.

**7** Repeat step 6 for this side too.

**8** Working with the front layer, open it a little bit and along the existing fold-lines, inside reverse fold the side point into the model.

Heart Balloon © 2014 Yuri Shumakov

9

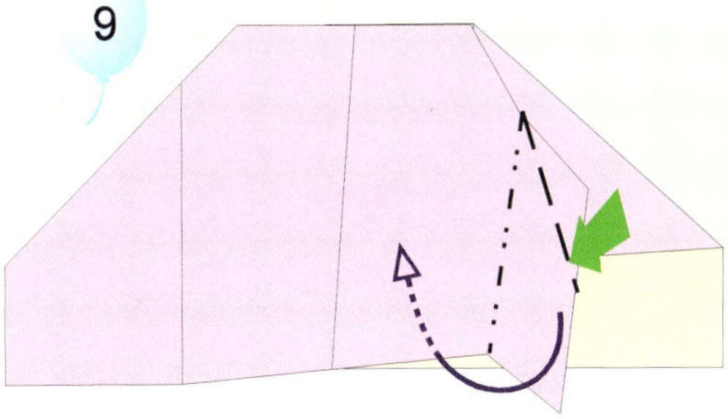

Repeat steps 8-9 with left-hand
side, thereby inside reverse fold
the side point into the model.

10

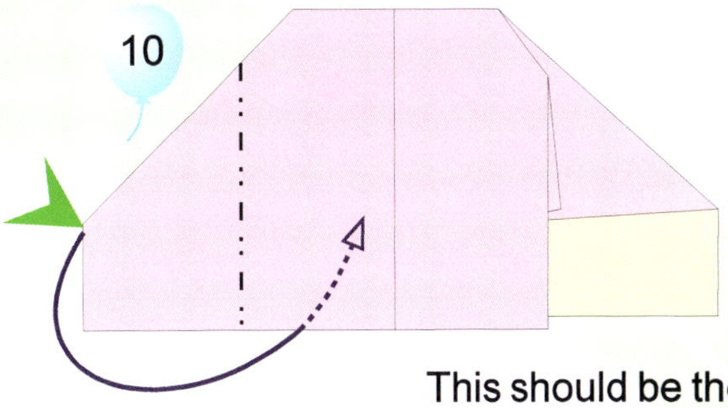

In the process.

This should be the result.
Now turn the model over
from side to side.

11

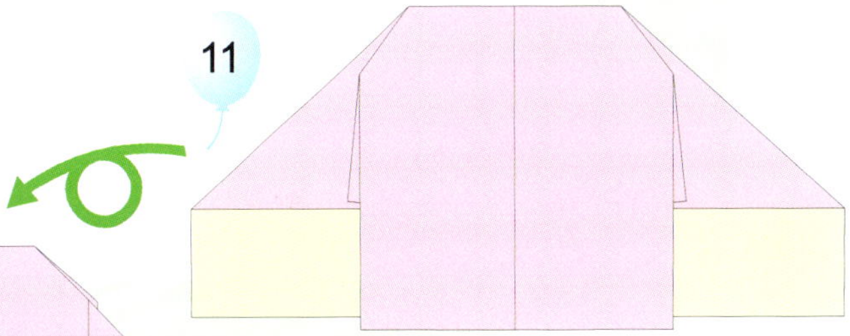

Repeat steps 8-10
for this side too.

12

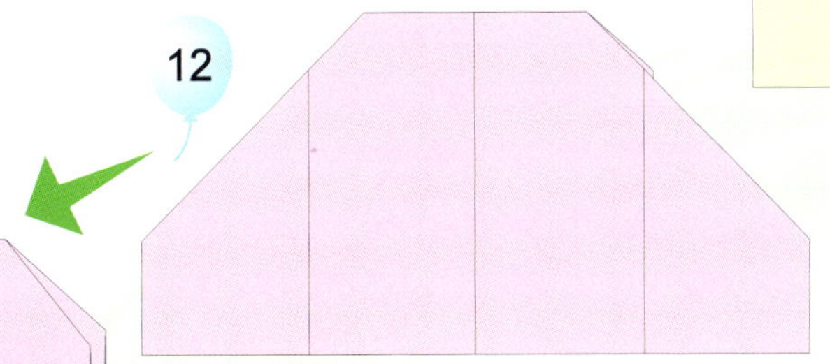

13 This should be
the result.

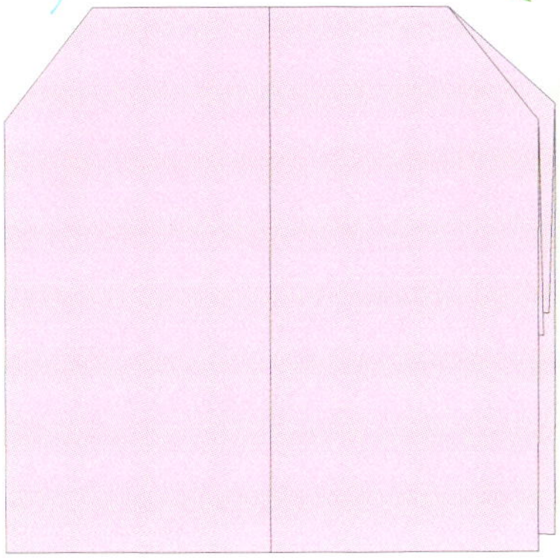

The following steps are shown
as the photo-diagrams.

14

Take the model and turn it around into the position
shown in the next step.

15

This should be the result. Gently open the sides,
so that the upper part remains compressed.

Heart Balloon © 2014 Yuri Shumakov

16

Turn the model toward you. Working with the upper part, gently push the left-hand side of the open folds, so that the layers coincide as shown in the next step.

17

This should be the result. Now push the layers into the model, re-forming the vertical middle line into a 'valley'.

18

This should be the result. Close the sides a bit, so that the layers are alighted inside.

19

Now turn the model around and repeat steps 16-18 for the other open folds.

20

Now close the side flaps and return the model into the initial position.

21

This should be the result. The layers inside are locked.
The following steps are shown in the vector diagrams.

Heart Balloon © 2014 Yuri Shumakov

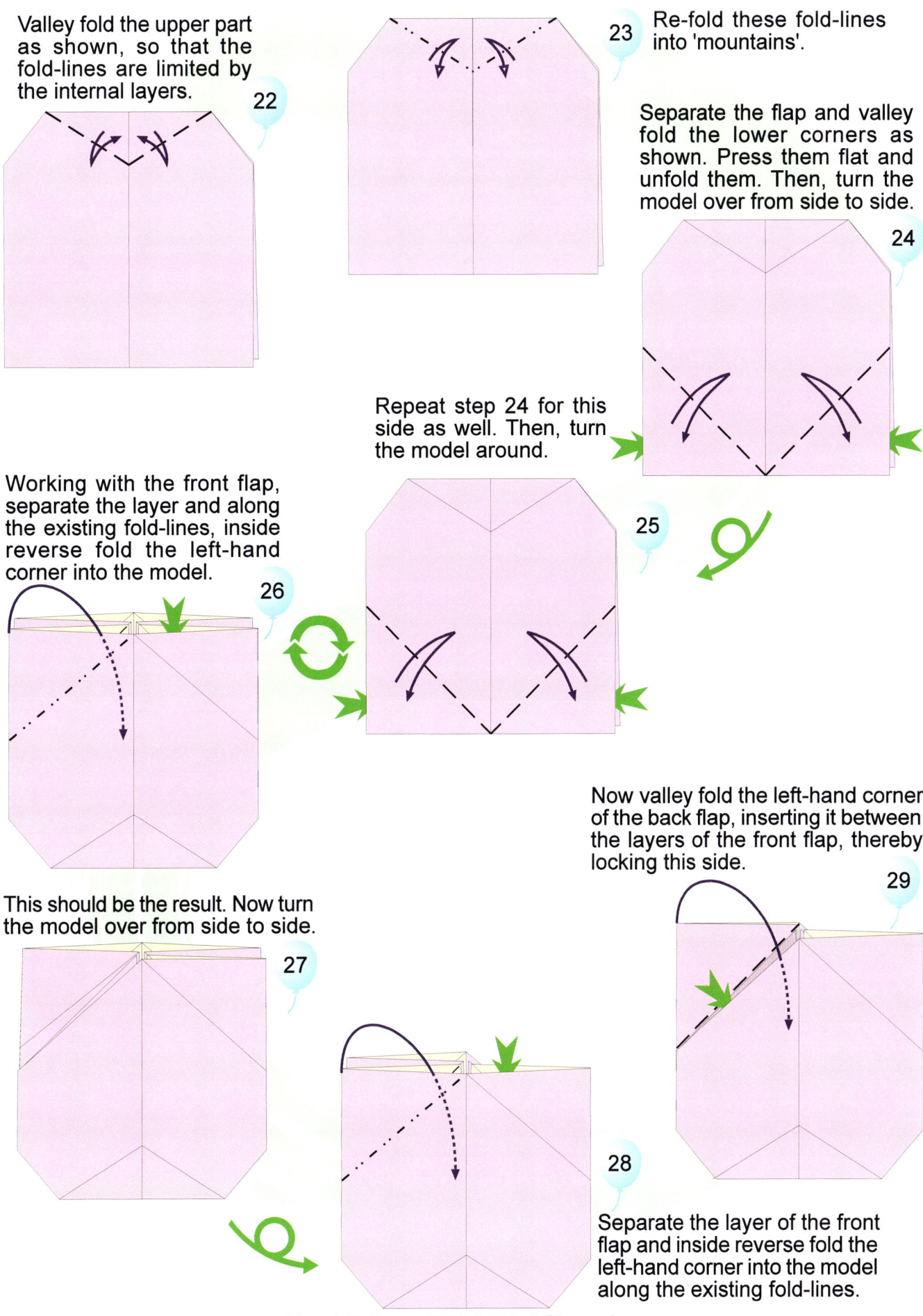

Valley fold the upper part as shown, so that the fold-lines are limited by the internal layers.

22

23 Re-fold these fold-lines into 'mountains'.

Separate the flap and valley fold the lower corners as shown. Press them flat and unfold them. Then, turn the model over from side to side.

24

Repeat step 24 for this side as well. Then, turn the model around.

25

Working with the front flap, separate the layer and along the existing fold-lines, inside reverse fold the left-hand corner into the model.

26

This should be the result. Now turn the model over from side to side.

27

Now valley fold the left-hand corner of the back flap, inserting it between the layers of the front flap, thereby locking this side.

29

28

Separate the layer of the front flap and inside reverse fold the left-hand corner into the model along the existing fold-lines.

Heart Balloon © 2014 Yuri Shumakov

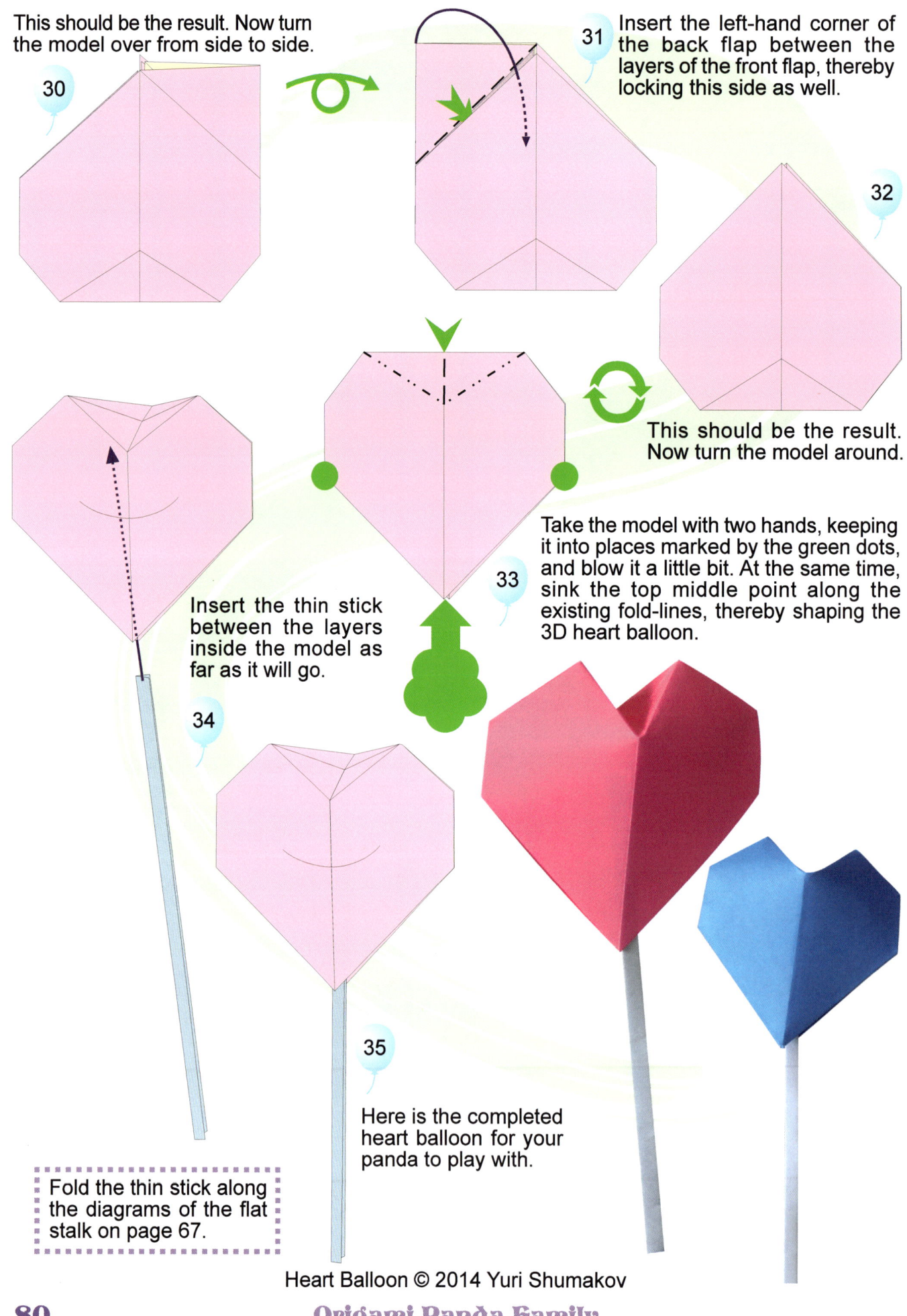

This should be the result. Now turn the model over from side to side.

30

31 Insert the left-hand corner of the back flap between the layers of the front flap, thereby locking this side as well.

32

This should be the result. Now turn the model around.

Take the model with two hands, keeping it into places marked by the green dots, and blow it a little bit. At the same time, sink the top middle point along the existing fold-lines, thereby shaping the 3D heart balloon.

33

Insert the thin stick between the layers inside the model as far as it will go.

34

35

Here is the completed heart balloon for your panda to play with.

Fold the thin stick along the diagrams of the flat stalk on page 67.

Heart Balloon © 2014 Yuri Shumakov

Origami Panda Family

# About Authors

**Y**uri and Katrin Shumakov - a stellar artist-duo, professional origami creators, who started their origami journey in France in 1989 and since then unfold this art in a heretofore unseen way!

They have created amazing paper world ORILAND with incredible fantasy Kingdoms that impress with rich detail of majestic castles, abundance of paper flora and busy life of little paper dwellers. Their newest kingdoms Toy-ronto and Albuquerque combine fantasy and reality together, presenting a whimsical artistic rendition of iconic sights of these cities.

*Oriland Exhibition, Stony Brook, NY, USA, 2002.*

*Miniature Oribana 'Tea Time'*

Another beautiful and elegant aspect of origami they brought to life is ORIBANA - a marriage of two Japanese arts: Origami and Ikebana. By combining these remarkable art-forms, in early 1990s Katrin and Yuri began to create paper flower arrangements in paper vases and thought up a distinctive name for it - Oribana. Since then they designed more than 50 charming oribana-compositions with a broad variety of origami flowers, leaves and vases.

Being prolific origami authors they created more than a thousand of origami designs from simple forms and cute characters to complex dinosaurs' skeletons and architecture that all have a distinctive Oriland style. Their Oriland Magic Star is a big action origami hit that amazes and dazzles with its mesmerizing effect when rotated.

*Oriland's TOY-RONTO Kingdom, Canadian National Exhibition, Toronto, ON, Canada, 2013.*

*Oriland's Albuquerque Kingdom, Albuquerque, NM, USA, 2013.*

Psychologists by education, Katrin and Yuri Shumakov have studied how origami helps children learn. Their Ph.D scientific work shows that by doing origami, children develop better use of both hands, whether they are left- or right- handed. They also discovered that origami can improve creativity and intelligence in children ages 7 to 11. They believe that origami is "entertainment for the soul, gymnastics for the mind, and training for the hands."

In 1999, Yuri and Katrin received the Silver Award in the ThinkQuest International Competition for their 'Travel to Oriland' website and it brought them and their team to Universal Studios Hollywood for the Award Ceremony! Their Oriland.com website became a winner of the Childnet Award that was given them in Paris, France. Both these projects were acknowledged as high quality creative, educational and fun websites for children and adults.

Yuri and Katrin have written more than 30 origami books and instructional CDs, and their works have been exhibited in many countries including several venues in the United States, France, Spain and Canada.

The Shumakovs also extend their artistic talents to the realm of photography and music. Katrin is a winner of the Toronto Photo Contest 2010; her photo art-works were recently exhibited across Canada. Yuri is enjoying music composing and sound design; he has released eight music albums in Space, Ambient, New Age and Smooth Jazz genres.

Katrin and Yuri live in Toronto, Canada, love yoga and a healthy style of life.

Visit their Oriland website to
see what origami can be!
http://www.oriland.com

Join Oriland on Facebook
https://www.facebook.com/oriland.fb

Follow Oriland on Twitter
https://twitter.com/Oriland

*Origami Montgolfier Balloon*

*Oriland Magic Star*

Printed in Great Britain
by Amazon.co.uk, Ltd.,
Marston Gate.